The PAINSPOTTER'S Guide To BROKEN BRITAIN

Andrew Holmes & Dan Wilson

CAPSTONE

This edition first published 2009
© 2009 Andrew Holmes and Dan Wilson

Registered office
Capstone Publishing Ltd. (A Wiley Company), The Atrium, Southern Gate, Chichester, West Sussex, PO19 8SQ, United Kingdom

For details of our global editorial offices, for customer services and for information about how to apply for permission to reuse the copyright material in this book please see our website at www.wiley.com.

Wiley also publishes its books in a variety of electronic formats. Some content that appears in print may not be available in electronic books.

Designations used by companies to distinguish their products are often claimed as trademarks. All brand names and product names used in this book are trade names, service marks, trademarks or registered trademarks of their respective owners. The publisher is not associated with any product or vendor mentioned in this book. This publication is designed to provide accurate and authoritative information in regard to the subject matter covered. It is sold on the understanding that the publisher is not engaged in rendering professional services. If professional advice or other expert assistance is required, the services of a competent professional should be sought.

The views expressed in this book are solely those of the authors and do not reflect the opinions of either Capstone Publishing or John Wiley & Sons Ltd.

Library of Congress Cataloguing-in-Publication Data (to follow)

9781906465711

A catalogue record for this book is available from the British Library.

Set in 9 on 11pt Fontana NDE by SNP Best-set Typesetter Ltd., Hong Kong
Printed in Great Britain by TJ international Ltd. Padstow

To Gordon Brown – without whom this book would not have been necessary

Contents

The end of boom and bust

I have been watching this recession arrive for quite some time and I am certainly not surprised that it is here or indeed at its severity. For at least the last four years, I have been reading books, newspaper articles and blogs which have been warning of the impending doom. As time wore on these became more and more alarmist in their claims and predictions and although sometimes very enjoyable to read, they were clearly depressing. And unlike the apparent threat from 'Y2K' which was going to wipe out civilisation, this current economic turmoil may actually succeed.

It should have been obvious to anyone who has the reading age of an illiterate that things were getting out of hand. But clearly people cannot read or were just too busy spending like water and juggling their credit card debt to notice. But the supreme irony has been in the actions of our elected officials who have expertly demonstrated that not only are they out of touch with what is happening economically, but they are also patently unable to organise a bun fight in a bakery. Claiming to have banished boom and bust to 'the dustbin of economic history' is something that only a moron would do, or perhaps an alien from a distant galaxy newly arrived on planet Earth; at least they could be forgiven. Of course it gets worse, as having spent recklessly for a decade there is now nothing left in the coffers to get us out of this mess. So the answer is to saturate the markets with more cash (euphemistically known as 'quantitative easing') and saddle the next ten generations with massive amounts of debt, (tax, tax and more tax). Apart from the chosen few (the politicians, their friends, the mega-rich, high-rolling bankers and a few ex-CEOs of screwed up banks), no one is being spared the misery of their economic incompetence.

Of course, it is not only the politicians we have to blame. Celebrities, too, have much to answer for with their obsession for empty-headed wealth generation, an approach that most of the population has seemingly bought into, despite having no celebrity and very little wealth. The public's spending spree has finally hit a brick wall. There are millions of people who have been caught with their pants down and have woken up to a massive debt hangover that even a good dose of Alka-Seltzer won't cure. Many of course have only themselves to blame.

But no matter how bad it gets, the one thing we do have is the ability to laugh in the face of adversity; some good old fashioned 'Blitz Spirit', a bit of 'Shadenfreude', is what's needed – it's always good to laugh at other peoples' misery rather than your own. So instead of taking that piece of razor wire to your femoral artery, please read this book. In it you will find the antidote to all your woes and if nothing else it will provide you with the comforting knowledge that you are not alone. It's cheaper than Prozac and less addictive.

AH

Acknowledgements

This book would not have been possible without the incompetence, greed, stupidity and arrogance of so many people, way too many to mention. However, there a few I would like to thank from the bottom of my wallet, my empty pension pot and for my children's hamstrung, debt ridden future. Without them this book would have never been possible. So, in no particular order I would like to thank Gordon Brown, Yvette Cooper, Alistair Darling, Alan Greenspan, George Bush, Bernie Madoff, Fred Goodwin, Jacqui Smith, New Labour, Lehman Brothers, AIG, The Royal Bank of Scotland (sorry, England), the G20, mortgage brokers, estate agents, the rocket scientists working in the investment banks, and everyone who's lived well beyond their means for the last 20 years. I have appreciated your invaluable input.

There are of course a small number of people who are genuinely worthy of acknowledgement for their input, support and feedback during the writing of this book. Emma Swaisland and the Capstone team; it's good to be back; Dan Wilson, who as always produces such superb images to complement the entries so well and which always make me laugh; Graham Guest and his interesting and now groundbreaking views on quantum finance; David Mitchell, with whom I laughed like a drain when we discussed potential entries; David Vaughan and Colin Woolgar, with whom I discussed the merits of abattoir sets for recently bereaved middle class girls who had to kiss goodbye to their beloved pony; and, of course, my family who are always delighted to see me back at my laptop writing yet another bloody book!

AH

Let the bad times roll

It's only when the tide goes out that you learn who's been swimming naked – *Warren Buffett*

Recession 101

During the 1980s when I was barely into my teenage years we found ourselves in the depth of a deep and very painful recession. The one thing that stuck out amongst it all, apart from the incessant strikes, riots and power cuts of course, was the way the news broadcasts would highlight the latest job cuts announced each day. The deadpan and serious delivery of the news, that another 7500 people had just been made redundant from a steelworks in the North of England, was accompanied by a colourful looking starburst which contained the jobless total carefully positioned over the approximate location where the redundancies took place. Alongside the map of the UK was a counter that would indicate the running total of those who were out of work. Up, up and up it went. Admittedly it looked a bit naff, but I guess that's all they could do before PowerPoint. This time around the deadpan newsreader has been replaced by a pseudo-celebrity arm-waving cretin who can't even speak in complete sentences and whose latest job losses announcement is accompanied by a satellite image zooming in from outer space, sometimes from beyond the solar system, pinpointing with extreme accuracy the precise location of the office where the redundancy letters were signed.

We have, of course, been subject to the vagaries of the economic cycle ever since we dragged ourselves out of the primordial soup. Back then, the cycle was defined by the availability of edible flora and fauna, whilst today it is principally about spending and debt. Even during the short time I have been alive there have been a few booms and busts, a couple of v-shaped recoveries as well as u-shaped and jobless recoveries too. There have been periods of high inflation and high interest rates and times when interest rates and inflation were low. I guess the only thing I have not lived through is a depression, but according to some we are heading that way so maybe I will be able to chalk that one up to experience too.

Recessions and indeed depressions come and go; some are long and some are short, but they are nearly always nasty in one way, shape or form. And although there are those who believe that they have solved the old problems associated with boom and bust, it is well known amongst the Scientologist community that it is only aliens from outer space who can do this type of thing and although the chancellor resembles an alien, he doesn't act like one. Sometimes recessions are bad for a single cohort of society and occasionally they affect each and every one of us whether directly or indirectly. This one, however, seems to be especially bad and not only is it impacting most of the population (it doesn't really matter if you are a homeowner, a pensioner, in work or out of work), but it is also likely to run and run and run.

We should remember that this is a global recession impacting countries across the world which is good news as it gives our leaders someone else to blame. What beggars belief, however, is that the supposed 'experts' and government officials who were on the economic frontline and meant to be monitoring the economy were not forecasting any downtown at all, and if they were, only a very shallow contraction. In doing so they have demonstrated that they are unfit for their jobs. But, as we know most of those who seek government office are self-centred, ego driven maniacs with no real concept of what is going on in the world outside the petty arguments and pointless debates that fill their day.

What goes up must come down

The boom since the last recession of the early 1990s seemed to be unstoppable, and despite the brief dip following the bursting of the Dotcom bubble continued unabated. However, it has now gone into reverse at an alarming speed. Starting with the collapse of Bear Sterns, the news around the world has got progressively worse. We have witnessed the failure of a significant number of banks who have either been subsumed by other institutions or have been bailed out and nationalised – it seems we are all bankers these days; what a terrible thought.

Any industry sector that relied on the out-of-control spending of consumers is suffering and experiencing double digit drops in demand, revenue and profits. And for some it has resulted in them going to wall in the most spectacular, and sadly inevitable, car crash that occurs when the music stops.

The financial markets have been decimated along with the pension pots and savings of millions who were told that the sure-fire investments they were making would see them right. Unemployment continues to ratchet up to levels we have not seen for many years and who knows which may yet reach levels not witnessed since the Great Depression. Companies and people are going bankrupt as their precarious financial positions have got to the point where only a big lottery win would get them out of the hole they're in.

Times are likely to be tough for a very long while yet and far longer than the morons who have been running the country since 1997 would like us to believe. Even looking at it from the simple perspective of government debt, we are deep in the mire. Government borrowing started way back in 1692 and it took 300 years for this to reach £165 billion. It has taken New Labour barely 18 months to rack up the same level, which means that someone born today will be 23 before it is back to sustainable levels. Nice job.

It's not my fault, honest

So who's to blame? Well, the list is a long one, so I will keep it to a few of those who are worthy of special treatment.

There is no doubt that the idiots in power, the tax-obsessed left wing muppets who have wasted most of our taxes on pointless jobs, allowances for hardworking MPs and projects which were never going anywhere from the get-go, have a lot to answer for. They show no real concern about our plight and when they do they come across as arrogant, patronising and completely out of touch. They tell us that it will be alright and then tax us until we cough up blood, which they also tax. They talk about making efficiency savings across the bloated public sector, and then continue to increase it and pay themselves more.

Defeating Napoleon, Kaiser Wilhelm and Adolf Hitler almost bankrupted the country but the economic geniuses of New Labour look as though they will achieve what years of warfare failed to do; and still they smile, laugh and joke. It's a real shame we don't live in medieval times, as most of government would find themselves on the end of the tip of a very sharp sword or perhaps a blunt farm implement. Still it's nice to fantasise about them queuing up to be eviscerated. It would certainly draw a large crowd and provide some much needed entertainment.

Next on the list is the banking community and especially those that were apparently paid very handsomely to run them. Driven by insatiable greed, they developed more and more risky approaches to squeezing every last drop of profit from their increasingly complex, rocket-scientist-developed products. When they dreamt up collateralised debt and the opportunity to slice and dice consumer and corporate loans and sell them off to unsuspecting investors across the world, the final nail in the coffin of the boom was hammered home. Once the house of cards started to collapse no one knew who owed what to whom and who would pay the debts that had been racked up by simpleton consumers and corporations and passed off as a great investment opportunity to the rich and wealthy. Then when bank losses skyrocketed and the big bosses floored, it was the bank of you and I that was left to pick up the pieces.

Third on the list, and I promise I won't go on for much longer, is the general public. Now I grew up to believe that you had to live within your means and that it generally wasn't a good idea to get yourself too much into debt. So, being a good boy, I always ensured that my mortgage was never more than three times my income and put aside some cash for my retirement and for a rainy day. I took on some debt when I had to, but again this was paid off as quickly as possible so that I didn't feel burdened by it all. Such prudence (sorry to use a term often used to describe our former, now discredited chancellor and unelected prime minister) does in the long run pay off. I also believed in the good old protestant work ethic and that work was an unfortunate means to an end. However, to do all this meant shunning a bullshit celebrity culture in which everyone wants to be rich and famous, not going on crazy spending sprees buying overpriced tripe and not filling up my house with stuff I never needed in the first place. Clearly, few people did the same. As the television spewed-out more cheap reality TV shows and 'talent' competitions in which the witless and great unwashed tried to impress a bunch of cheesy and disinterested celebs with their (previously unrecognised) ability to tap dance or eat razor wire, the desire to work hard for a living went out the window. It became all about being the next Britney Spears or Paris Hilton. At the same time, those who clearly were talentless and would never become famous felt they shouldn't miss out on the celebrity lifestyle either. They went on a decade-long spending binge, maxing-out on their credit cards and using their houses as convenient piggy banks. And what have they got to show for it? Apart from an out-of-town lock-up stuffed full of the crap they bought and never use, huge amounts of debt, no savings and plenty of sleepness nights.

Pay up and look big

And who pays? Yes you've guessed it, it's us. With the government coffers running on empty and the public debt at unprecedented levels, ours, our children's, our children's, children's and our children's, children's, children's futures have been sold down the river. It will take generations to dig us out of the hole that we find ourselves in and we can only look forward to being taxed to death to pay for it. And don't expect any respite soon; there will be no return to boom, just perpetual bust dressed up as 'green shoots'. And when it comes to the cost of living and taxes, as Yaz said during the 1980's recession, 'The only way is up'.

Don't despair ... the perfect antidote is here

If you are anything like me, your blood must be boiling, but we all know that anger is not a helpful emotion because it has a range of detrimental effects. First and foremost, it forces your brain to shutdown as your Neanderthal need to beat the living daylights out of those to blame takes over from your higher performing frontal lobes which would allow you to have a reasonable discussion with Mr Brown, eruditely pointing out the error of his ways. Next, it does little for your long-term health as it plays all sorts of havoc with your blood pressure, leading to heart disease and strokes. Finally, it usually leads to a prison sentence, although I am sure in some cases your crimes will be looked upon in a sympathetic light by a judge who has also been taken to the cleaners.

So, now that we have established that it's all gone 'a bit Pete Tong', it's time to lighten up and use this very handy guide (at a true Credit Crunch beating price of course) to ease your pain and laugh at the sheer stupidity of it all. Consider it the like the latter day 'Blitz Spirit' when we could laugh like drains as the Luftwaffe dropped their latest payload of high explosives on the towns and cities of Britain.

In this book you will find fifty people who have either:

- got us into this almighty mess;
- been impacted by it all and never stop moaning;
- got away without being unduly affected, but deserve our vitriol anyway;
- or screwed up royally and are now in a terrible pickle.

For the experienced 'Painspotters' amongst the readership, you will know how to use this book. But for those who don't, it is designed in a way that allows you to identify the people associated with the Credit Crunch and ensuing recession – whether it is those who have done the crunching or those who have been well and truly crunched – whilst enabling you to express your inner feelings in an acceptable way. I am writing what you are thinking. Thus, in the same way that bird spotters identify the lesser spotted warbler, this book helps you to spot the Gravy Train Politician, the Ponzi Schemer, the Pissed-off state Pensioner and the Secure Civil Servant. But it goes beyond that, it identifies how you can avoid them and seek your revenge; if you are brave enough.

Each entry includes:

 Sympathy Rating – how much should we feel sorry for them? Extending from 0 (absolutely no sympathy whatsoever) to 10 (extreme sympathy to the point of tears, if not cash handouts).

 Rarity – ranging from 1 (exceptionally rare) to 10 (all too common).

 What are they doing now? That the recession is well and truly underway.

 Avoidance / revenge strategies (with suitable escalation).

At the end of each entry I have also given you, the reader, the opportunity to record them, add your own sympathy rating if you believe I have been too harsh (or perhaps too lenient), and to decide who is ultimately blameworthy.

As with any 'spotting' pastime, you might choose to swap entries with your friends and families or, God forbid, your local MP. You might also choose to throw the book through the front windows of any fat cat residences that happen to be down your street. And I am sure that you will be 'Twittering' your thoughts and reactions online. And Dan and I hope to see you on the Painspotting website: www.Painspotting.co.uk

Sadly, you could be referring to this book over the many years this recession is likely to last, but I hope you will be using it to cheer yourself up. I would also recommend that you consider bequeathing this to your children or grandchildren, as I am sure they will be needing it too. Who needs self-help books, when armed with this tome, you can simply avoid the jerks, muppets and morons who make life such a drag?

Fellow Painspotters, let us begin ...

The About to Retire, Retiree

Believe it or not, there are a few people out there who love the whole concept of work and believe that all retirement means is the long (or short) slide to death, filled with endless wood turning and existential discussions with the local vicar. I actually believe work is more like death than retirement could ever be. Let's face it, being stuck in an office at your desk or the cockpit of a Boeing 777 doing the same thing day after day, after day is mind numbing and also pretty soul destroying. Ultimately work should be a means to an end which hopefully isn't just death. Those who believe that work is the only thing that matters are seriously deluded and need psychological counselling. Retirement is and should be something to be looked forward to and savoured, ideally embarked upon at the earliest opportunity. Indeed, according to all the advertisements for pension savings, it is a time for renewal and the last opportunity to pursue all those hobbies and pastimes that you never could whilst working inhuman hours for a complete and utter bastard.

Just picture it. You have spent somewhere in the region of 30 or perhaps 40 years giving your life and soul to a single employer or perhaps a series of companies. You have worked hard, diligently meeting every target that's ever been set. You have laughed at your boss' crap jokes, perhaps even had sex with him or her to secure that much coveted promotion, suffered the backstabbing of your colleagues, watched as incompetent idiots climb the greasy pole as you and your supreme talents have been overlooked, and dealt with difficult clients who have treated you like rubbish. All this has been worth it because you knew that at some point in the future it would all come to an end. Then you could kick back and never have to deal with morons ever again, comfortable in the knowledge that you or your employer or perhaps both had squirreled enough cash aside to get you through to the inevitable death rattle. Well, so you thought.

The unfortunate thing for so many almost retired workers is that their seemingly surefire, concrete plans have turned to dust. Retirement for many is now no longer a fantasy but more like a fairytale. The problems which started with the collapse of Bear Sterns have worsened with every unfortunate lurch of the Credit Crunch and subsequent recession, from being fleeced by the likes of Bernie Madoff to companies going to the wall and refusing to pay out one dime of their pension pots. And, even if you have not lost absolutely everything to one of the many 'Ponzis' out there, your pension pot is likely to be a shadow of its former self. And although the investment management community loves to tell everyone that it is important to hang on, for many people approaching retirement, hanging on means a death sentence. As you would expect, the government has done us no favours – in truth, they screwed up pensions years ago. And let me think who that might have been …. ah yes, Gordon Brown, that 'safe pair of hands' and economic genius. With quantitative easing adding to the misery as it drives down annuity rates, things are unlikely to improve for the near-retiree or even distant-retiree anytime this side of the next millennium. The I'm About to Retire, Retiree typically

wears a hangdog expression and rarely smiles. With their dreams in tatters you can see them on the train station platforms every morning looking depressed and resigned to another ten years of work. Their wives however, are delighted because they can continue to enjoy life, happy in the knowledge that their dull work-centric husband won't be hanging around them like a stain for at least another decade.

Tales of poor 60–65 year old workers who can no longer afford to retire are everywhere. It won't be long before we'll see white haired rioters taking to the streets brandishing their walking sticks and bus passes, all in desperate need of the lavatory. I do, however, see two silver linings to the whole debacle. First, every near-retiree should seek a new job in a new company, and when they are turned down sue the pants of them so that they can replenish their pension pots and retire anyway. This of course is now possible with the new age discrimination legislation and if you can throw in a bit of sexual or racial discrimination too, then all the better. The second, which is aimed at those with a few years to run before they can retire, is that with so many old people in work and the associated delays to retirement, annuity rates are bound to increase as the time between retiring and death will become much shorter. I know it is a bit of a sacrifice, but it is important to think about the next generation. Indeed, I actually think this whole credit crunch thing has been deliberately engineered by governments across the world to avoid having to pay out the pensions of the gazillions of baby boomers who are on the cusp of retiring. Gordon, I take it all back, you are indeed a financial genius.

☐ **Tick here when you have spotted the About to Retire, Retiree**

SYMPATHY RATING – **10**

As someone who would love to retire tomorrow given the chance and who saves like crazy so that I will actually be able to retire in relative comfort, (assuming my pension pot recovers, of which there is no guarantee), I have enormous sympathy for anyone who has lost out due to the incompetence of the government and investment management community. What makes us really angry is that the bankers who brought down the finance system have walked away with massive payoffs and huge pensions so that they will never have to work again. Not that they could, why would anyone with a CV containing an entry such as '2004–2008 CEO of ABC Bank plc – over the course of my tenure at the bank, I destroyed the company's capital base, took reckless risks with other people's money and had to ask the government to nationalise the company because of my almighty cock-up' be considered an asset ever again? Apart from a toxic asset, of course.

RARITY – **5**

With the population visibly aging before our eyes and with the recession likely to run for the foreseeable future, the numbers of the About to Retire, Retirees will continue to rise. You will see them everywhere; shops, offices, train stations, all foaming at the mouth as they bitch about those bastard bankers and evil politicians who have destroyed their future. Even the ones who only saved £56 to fund their retirement can't help but go off on one. I am not sure how this will impact the quality of service you might expect to receive from them, but I can only guess that it will be poor.

WHAT ARE THEY DOING NOW?

If not contemplating suicide or perhaps going berserk with an assault rifle, they are crying themselves to sleep as they flick through magazine pictures of tanned, grey-haired old men at the helms of their yachts knowing that will have to work at least another five or ten years and may never, ever be able to retire. The prospect of having to continue to work as they get increasingly infirm is not a wonderful one and once they finally finish it will be off to a grotty, publically funded care home where they will no doubt be beaten up by the staff. Hmm, maybe assisted suicide sounds like an option after all.

AVOIDANCE | REVENGE STRATEGIES

1. Forget about retiring, that's just for cissies and people who want to spend all afternoon sitting in an armchair rocking from side to side and occasionally passing wind. Work makes you strong and apparently is a sure fire way to live to well over 100.

2. It is best to think about the future at an early age and I would recommend that you start saving for your pension as soon as you start work; forget about the new sports car, think about the future.

3. If you happen to be getting towards retiring seek some professional advice from someone that knows about these things and aim to steer clear of risky assets on the run up to retirement. It seems that many didn't follow this sage advice and have been pole axed as a result.

4. Write to your MP demanding that the civil service pension scheme be extended to the whole population, as it is only fair that everyone who is workshy and not much use to society (including pensioners) should receive this very generous and unfunded benefit.

5. Write to the government and ask them to resurrect the Victorian Workhouse and open it for those about to retire. In return for their hard work offer them a hard bed and a cup of gruel at mealtimes. Compared to what they would be otherwise facing, this will seem like heaven.

THE ABOUT TO RETIRE, RETIREE:

☐ Can blame someone else for their predicament

☐ Only has them self to blame

☐ Deserves our sympathy and should be hugged

☐ Deserves our contempt and should be shot

The Bailout Beggar

The Credit Crunch has clearly left a lot of people and a lot of companies in dire straits and ever since it started we have been inundated with headlines claiming that the whole capitalist system is on the brink of collapse and unless we act soon, the world will literally end. Well in fact it is going to end, but not until 2012. According to Mayan prophesies, which are based upon two millennia of astronomical observations, the world will cease to exist on 21 December 2012, which will probably coincide with the end of the recession. If it did, it would be a real bummer for everyone. Mind you, for those mired in debt, it will probably come as a wonderful release – no more bailiffs, as they will die too. I do wonder, though, if your debts and indeed the Credit Crunch itself can pass to the other side; I guess we'll find out soon enough.

As things went from bad to worse and as politicians around the world stared into the headlights of economic Armageddon, there was a desperate need to do something, anything, to show that they were in control of events and not the other way around. Then, someone came up with a cunning plan and a cunning slogan – 'BAILOUT'. That's it they thought, rather than let everything go to the wall, let's splash some cash and make all the problems just go away, leaving it to the next generation to figure out how to sort out the crap. As we 'Generation X-ers' have been well and truly shafted by the Baby Boomers, now it's our turn to shaft the 'Generation Y-ers' – who kind of deserve it as few of them work, they spend all day on Facebook and like to complain that they have got it hard.

With the bailout a new beast was born: the Bailout Beggar. The Bailout Beggar is typically a company or corporation that has screwed up really, really, really badly to the point that if no one helped them they would go bust. So along they came, companies of all shapes and sizes, hands outstretched looking to get a few billion to tide them over and to help them pay a few bonuses to their overworked and underpaid staff. As the economic stimulus gathered pace and as governments pushed more and more money into the economy, the number of Bailout Beggars grew. It started-off with just the idiots who were at least 80% to blame for the mess in the first place – the banks. But they were soon joined by a whole bunch of CEOs, flying into Washington on their private jets to ask for a piece of the action. Some companies were left to die, and quite rightly so, as their business was rubbish anyway and should not have been allowed to continue. Others, like AIG were just too big to fail (or so we are told), as they really would have taken down the whole capitalist system and heralded the end of the world, much to the disgust of the Mayans no doubt. The money kept on flowing – a hundred billion for you, and a couple of billion for you. It was like Oliver Twist – 'please Sir, can I have some more?' and all we had to do was wait for Harry Secombe to break into song.

Banks were nationalised, insurance companies thrown lifelines and auto-manufacturers told to sod off. Then came the long line of beggars just like the ones who turn up on

your doorstep when you've won the lottery. The major industries were joined by sewage companies, cattle farmers, old peoples' homes, Wal-Mart and then, to top it all, the Porn Industry wanted to get some bailout cash as well. They didn't want that much compared to the rest of the Bailout Beggars, just a mere $5 billion. The amount reflected the decline in US 'adult industry' revenue from a peak of $18 billion three years ago. Apparently it's not only the economy that's sagging these days, actors and performers are finding their customer bases (amongst other things) shrinking, and the rates which porn stars are being paid per scene has dropped significantly to $1200 from $2000 – a girl just can't make a decent living lying on her back anymore. Clearly this industry is more deserving than the banks as it might be just what is needed to get the economy pumping again.

Of course, as soon as the money started flowing from central government, everyone, no matter how tenuous the link between their current predicament and the Credit Crunch really was, lined up to get some cash. Whether it was because they had invested their money in a bankrupt country like Iceland, or had gambled it away on hedge funds, it didn't really matter. And of course everyone believes they are just as entitled to the money as the evil, greedy, good-for-nothing, high-living, jet-setting, money-grabbing, unrepentant bankers. What's good for the goose is clearly good for the gander.

☐ **Tick here when you have spotted the Bailout Beggar**

SYMPATHY RATING – **6**
Most people are of course outraged that any company that has been as badly run as the banks or the auto manufacturers should be given a handout. Let them all fail, after all there are plenty of businesses going to the wall because of the Credit Crunch, and they get jack; just a blank expression from a government official. However, attempting to take a broader view of events, you can see the need to keep some of the companies going because they employ millions of people, and the systemic risk of them taking down the entire nation is a very real one. Still if I were you, I would be venting your spleen in one of the many riots that have been taking place across the world.

RARITY – **9**
There are more Bailout Beggars than you can shake a stick at right now, and as long as the Credit Crunch and recession continues, companies will continue to queue up for their slice of the bailout pie. Heck, I might even try myself ... if you don't ask, you don't get.

WHAT ARE THEY DOING NOW?
Spending the bailout cash on new corporate jets, paying out big chunks of it to their workers to keep them happy and to stop them from being sued,

and, oh yes, using a small portion to stimulate the economy by getting consumers to spend again. Now wasn't it that which got us into this mess in the first place?

AVOIDANCE | REVENGE STRATEGIES
1. Sit back and let the whole thing wash over you, comfortable in the knowledge that those in authority must know what they are doing.

2. Make the most of the Bailout Beggar's attempt at getting you to spend money again by picking up a cheap mortgage or a nice new GM car at third world prices.

3. Stage a West End Musical called Bailout. See if you can get a few of the sacked (but still wealthy) CEOs to star in it and Andrew Lloyd Webber to write it.

4. Join one of the many protests seeking to destroy capitalism and all of its excesses. I would recommend any anarchist group, as they tend to have the best slogans and I rather like their black outfits.

5. Seek some of the bailout money for yourself and if you are successful, treat yourself to two weeks in the Caribbean.

THE BAILOUT BEGGAR:

☐ Can blame someone else for their predicament

☐ Only has them self to blame

☐ Deserves our sympathy and should be hugged

☐ Deserves our contempt and should be shot

The Buy-to-Let Basket Case

For years and years and years we have had to endure insufferable bores and their obsession with property. I can only believe that there must have been some kind of virus in the air or perhaps some radioactive chemical had leaked into the water supply. No matter where you turned or who you talked to, the only topic of conversation was 'the property market'. Forget about having an erudite discussion on the major issues of the day, the only thing that mattered was how much their property was worth, or how they no longer invested in their pension because the only way to make any decent returns these days was through your property – and pensions were soooo 19th Century. I have to say that I could never understand the logic of such statements. So, here you are having worked hard to secure a nice home with plenty of room and then retirement comes along. Because you have failed to invest in anything apart from your lovely home, you have no choice but to move out ('downshift' as it is known), most likely to a tiny bedsit as you need the remaining cash to fund your retirement. With all your worldly possessions stacked floor to ceiling around you, you finally realise that maybe it wasn't such a smart move after all especially as you have barely enough room to swing a rat and that the £45.67 per week you have to live off won't see you through to your inevitable demise. The only word that springs to mind is cretin.

Then there were the fatuous and seemingly unending television shows about property – at least half the viewing schedule was clogged up with show after show showing us either how to buy or how to 'improve' our homes. For a nation of net curtain-twitchers, it was a winning format. E-listed celebrities infested the small screen helping the latest clutch of idiots attempt to turn a profit on some rundown three-bed semi on the outskirts of Prestatyn. The self-appointed property experts would dish out important advice on how to convert a dump into a goldmine and how to live off the proceeds. Then there were the shows which involved following hapless former teachers and lap dancers as they attempted to renovate randomly selected houses, ignoring all the advice from architects, builders and of course the Planning Department, usually with disastrous results. And once they had completed the work (typically way over budget and to an inferior quality), a succession of shiny-suited estate agents would give their opinion (like it ever counted for much) as the amateur developers stood by and bit their nails. Having made a couple of thousand in profit, the now experienced property developers would move onto their next project confident in their abilities to retire rich and spend their dotage in the Caribbean rubbing shoulders with people like Tony Blair and Cliff Richard.

It's really no surprise. The property obsession was fueled by the continuous rise in property prices that went on year after year and seemed to be the most surefire

investment since Bernie Madoff's great Ponzi scheme. The middle classes in particular loved the idea of getting rich off their houses, as it gave them something else to boast about apart from how talented their children were. Social climbing reached new heights with property becoming the new battlefield in one-upmanship between competing middle class bores desperate to show their net worth was larger than their friends and families. Soon, households found themselves mired in debt as their buy-to-let empires grew and grew. Realising that the rental income would barely cover their mortgage payments, they would tell those who could be bothered to listen that they were in it for capital growth and that the income didn't matter; just as well.

Then the Credit Crunch came along and the bottom fell out of the housing market. The Buy-to-Let Boaster soon became the Buy-to-Let Basket Case or perhaps more appropriately the Buy-to-Lose Loser. Not only have property prices crashed to the point where all the amazing gains have gone, but there are now so many buy-to-let properties on the market that tenants are forcing down rents. The outgoings from all their rental properties are exceeding rental income and capital growth. Instead of making money they are now losing it hand over fist. So what do they tell their friends now? 'Oh well, I kind of f***ed up, but at least I have an empire of 45 properties which have no tenants and which are losing money year on year. The market will soon pick up ...' Only to make matters worse, lenders are asking for massive repayments to cover the loss of capital in properties, and the government wants the '1 million or so' landlords to be registered and follow a bunch of mind numbing rules, (no doubt enforced by The Landlord Police who would have the power to revoke the licence and send all the landlord's tenants packing).

As desperation sets in, the Buy-to-Let Basket Case fire-sells their properties at auction to stay one step ahead of their creditors, and I pity the poor tenants who wake up to the splintering of their front door as the bailiffs come in mob-handed, chucking them out on the street as they search for anything remotely valuable. Perhaps a video of Property Ladder might fetch a few bob at a jumble sale?

☐ **Tick here when you have spotted the Buy-to-Let Basket Case**

SYMPATHY RATING – 2
The whole property thing has been annoying from the get go. People have been delusional in their belief that property was the only investment in town and the only sure-fire route to retiring rich. Sure, every asset class is down the toilet right now, and there have been plenty of mugs drawn in by the odd Ponzi scheme or two, but property infected everyone and everything. There is a powerful sense of Shadenfreude right now, especially from those amongst the population who stood on the sidelines waiting for the whole thing to come crashing down. Now of course our middleclass friends claim to be in it for the long haul and they only bought the properties because they wanted to spend a bit of time there – places like Glasgow's East End, Toxteth and Stockport – yeah right. You see in the end, even with their property

investments crumbling around them, they still like to talk about property; how utterly one dimensional and dull.

RARITY - **8**

The Buy-to-Let Basket Case is very common and the professional property investors have recently been joined by a whole new bunch of would-be landlords – those who cannot sell their houses at the ridiculously high prices they were hoping to. So, instead of accepting an offer 30–50% lower than they need, they have joined the millions of amateur landlords. I just hope their tenants were a bit better than I was when I was a student – oh the mess.

WHAT ARE THEY DOING NOW?

Trying to figure out when their buy-to-let empire will ever make any money; with most of the properties tenantless and the capital well below the mortgage value, they finally understand the significance behind the Lost City of Atlantis.

AVOIDANCE | REVENGE STRATEGIES

1. Tell them that you only have one house and that it is to live in and is certainly not your pension. Or better still, tell them how you sold at the height of the market and are currently renting, 'waiting for a bargain to come up'.

2. Point them in the direction of www.housepricecrash.co.uk where they can see just how much money they have and continue to lose; it might bring them to their senses at last.

3. Lecture them on some basic economic principles, like supply and demand and investment cycles and throw in some simple Newtonian physics for good measure. Maybe they will understand that what goes up must come down.

4. Slap them around the face and tell them to get a grip – they have been very stupid and need to get their feet firmly back on the ground.

5. Place an advertisement in the national press asking for people to star in a new reality television programme called 'The Bailiffs are Coming' in which burly thugs break down the doors of various buy-to-let properties around the country.

THE BUY-TO-LET BASKET CASE:

☐ Can blame someone else for their predicament

☐ Only has them self to blame

☐ Deserves our sympathy and should be hugged

☐ Deserves our contempt and should be shot

The Cash Finder

The human race is a resourceful bunch and over the thousands of years since we actually did more than kill sabre tooth tigers and make the occasional fire – we have done some amazing things, like land on the moon, develop the computer and create reality TV shows. And now that the Credit Crunch is in full swing we are turning our amazing capabilities to finding cash. We have been told that cash is king for so long now that everyone outside of the corporate environment and those who are not qualified accountants appear to be embracing the concept and finding exciting ways of magic-ing cash out of thin air, often with the minimal amount of effort. If you are anything like most people, then you'll have squirreled away all those low value coins over the last ten or so years and when you realise that you have a stash of something in the region of £50000 in loose change, it's like winning the lottery, and in fact far better. Having looked myself, I have approximately £36 which admittedly is unlikely to get me through the recession. Apart from the obvious jars of coins and small pots of cash you might have dotted around the house, remember the few hundred quid that has fallen into, or behind the sofa, or the chance to cash-in at the local swimming baths by retrieving the money that has been left in the lockers, there are many other ways in which the Cash Finder is able to get hold of some readies and to save you the hassle of working these out yourself, here are the most effective ones:

• *Raiding your children's money boxes for anything you can find.* This is of course best done when they are asleep as you don't want to upset them before they go to bed; it's unfair and it will (a) give them nightmares; and (b) make them hate you for the rest of their lives. One of the best ways to achieve this is to throw their piggybank against the wall and stage a mock break-in. When they find that the little money they did have has gone, you can blame it on that casual visitor that came round last week (was it the vicar, or someone from the Women's Institute, you just can't remember). Or better still one of their brothers or sisters. Sure, there will be some tears but you can promise to investigate it all in the knowledge that once you get a new job you'll pay it all back (so no time soon).

• *Taking money out of the church collection plate/bag as it passed around the congregation.* This is perfectly acceptable given the church's traditional role of looking after paupers and those amongst their flock who are down on their luck. Of course you have to be a little bit careful. It's always a good idea to sit between a couple of old people who are partially blind but who tend to put lots of cash into the collection plate (hedging their bets with respect to their upcoming salvation by ingratiating themselves to their Lord no doubt). Just remember to pick out the Pound coins rather than the notes, as these tends to be less obvious even to the partially sighted, (plus notes rustle too much and can be easily spotted by the old bag two rows behind). If you are a regular churchgoer, then you ought to be able to maintain a healthy income. This may of course explain why church attendance has shot up since the recession started.

- *Selling your non-vital organs to the highest bidder.* This is a favourite amongst those who have found themselves in a lot of debt and who have also maintained a healthy lifestyle by following government guidelines on eating five portions of fruit and vegetables a day, steering clear of saturated fat, keeping a lid on the boozing and taking plenty of exercise. Kidneys are especially popular with Cash Finders because you have two of them and there is a strong demand.

- *Mugging the Big Issue seller and others who are good at collecting cash from the general public such as the do-gooders who collect change for charitable causes.* It is always a good idea to do this at the end of the day as by this time the haul is likely to be quite substantial, (well according to my lawyer friends who have done well out of it). And don't forget to make a donation yourself, as this is a nice way to show that you care.

Naturally not one to condone any kind of criminal behaviour it is also helpful to know that your fellow Cash Finders are discovering other ways to replace their lost income with some handy, non-taxable activities (after all, a cash society allows you to keep the tax authorities' thieving mitts off your money, especially as they have demonstrated just how recklessly they spend it). One of the most popular approaches in the UK is to riffle through your loft (or your grandma's) to see if there is anything valuable there. Ideally you ought to try to appear on that wonderful Credit Crunch programme – 'Cash in the Attic', as you get the support of an 'expert' antiques dealer who will maximise the price you get for all the old crap you find. In America, one of the most popular ways of getting extra cash is to go into stripping and the adult film industry. Apparently, employers across the adult entertainment industry are experiencing a surge of applications from women who are attracted by the promise of fast cash (sorry chaps, but it seems that they are less interested in you unless you happen to be incredibly well endowed). According to those that have made the leap, the money is good, although getting used to the five inch heels can be difficult – still, needs must.

☐ **Tick here when you have spotted the Cash Finder**

SYMPATHY RATING – 8
There is no doubt about it you have got to do the best you can to survive the recession and one of the best ways is to find as much cash as possible. It is a lovely experience to come across cash, and far better than any pay rise you might have been able to screw out of your tight-fisted employer. It is important to remember that difficult times call for difficult measures, so don't hold back now.

RARITY – 10
We are all Cash Finders these days and I would be surprised to hear about anyone who isn't. Of course, politicians are particularly good at finding cash out of the public purse and as a result have no problems at all paying for their everyday needs such as porn films and bath plugs.

WHAT ARE THEY DOING NOW?
Holding up the queue in the post office, petrol station or supermarket as they pay for everything in small change. As is usually the case, they never have quite enough money to complete the transaction and end up asking other people in the queue for the remaining 15 pence.

AVOIDANCE | REVENGE STRATEGIES
1. Children, charity workers and anyone else who has cash – make sure you keep a very close eye on your loose change and keep it under lock and key at all times.

2. Set yourself up as a Cash Finder guru and offer your services on a no-find, no-fee basis (a bit like the ambulance chasing lawyers which are advertised on television). Take 25% of any money you find.

3. Launch a TV programme called 'Cash in Your Freezer', in which members of the public sort though their freezers and select items to peddle around their local area. Watch in amazement as they collect thousands of pounds for a half eaten tub of Neapolitan ice cream.

4. Set yourself up as a latter-day Fagin and recruit a bunch of feral youths to be your street urchins. In return for somewhere safe to sleep, the said urchins will solicit cash from unsuspecting victims on the streets using a variety of cunning techniques reminiscent of the 19th century.

5. Set up an illegal printing press and create counterfeit bank notes and coins. Use elaborate designs and interesting denominations such as a thirty-five pound note and a seven pence coin. When challenged in the shops, tell them that the Chancellor has introduced some additional coinage and notes to beat the recession and to pay off the £175 billion public debt, it's all part of 'quantitative easing'.

THE CASH FINDER:

☐ Can blame someone else for their predicament

☐ Only has them self to blame

☐ Deserves our sympathy and should be hugged

☐ Deserves our contempt and should be shot

The Celebrity Money Saver

Anthropologists believe that there were celebrities even in the hunter gatherer societies of the Stone Age. Apparently those hunters that were better at bringing in the meat had younger and prettier women and were more often than not followed around by hordes of aspiring young men who obviously wanted the same. Some believe that these top hunters were obsessed about their reputations and liked to show off their spears to the other members of their tribe. Since that time celebrities have come and gone; you know people like Genghis Khan, Alexander the Great, Julius Caesar, and Adolf Hitler to name but a few. It was however, the advent of the telegraph, telephone and eventually the television that made celebrity what it is today. We now live in a world obsessed with celebrity and as a result have to endure mind-numbing television schedules packed with rubbish like 'American Idol', 'Pop Idol', 'Britain's got Talent' (really?), 'Dancing on Ice', 'The Apprentice' and other similarly cheaply made rubbish in which the great unwashed and self-obsessed pitch themselves against equally narcissistic egotists in the hope that they too will get the lucky break they deserve. Fortunately, most of them don't and end up having to work for a living in a job they hate, dealing with intense feelings of failure and self loathing. I am not a fan of the celebrity culture and I am certainly not a fan of all the cretins who play up to them and follow them around like lap dogs, all hoping for the celebrity stardust to rub off on to them.

But wait, according to a couple of American psychologists celebrities are actually wired differently from us normal people. As well as being incredibly vain and narcissistic, celebrities crave attention, are over confident in their abilities, lack empathy and behave erratically. And the fewer real skills they have the more desperate they are to hang onto the celebrity lifestyle. This helps to explain a lot, like why they could never survive in the real world, but it is no reason to cut them any slack – they should still be lined up against a wall and shot.

Because celebrities have an insatiable need to be in the limelight and to be the centre of attention, they will always be doing their utmost to find an angle that keeps them there. For example, despite having no background in or experience of the Middle East peace process, they will offer up their wisdom and thoughts to seasoned diplomats struggling to get the Arabs and Israelis to stop blowing each other up.

The Celebrity Money Saver is typically a C, D, E, or perhaps even F listed celebrity who feels that they should be imparting their infinite wisdom to an unsuspecting public. Turn on any daytime television chat show and there they are, telling the overly-enthusiastic presenter how people can save a few pence if they buy their book (£11.99 from all good bookshops …) on how to spend less. They cover everything from economising on food, ('introduce a 1940s-style rationing system in your house and live off bubble and squeak and rabbit pie'), through to clothing, ('can't your children wear moth-eaten garments from jumble sales or, their sister's hand-me-downs' – particularly

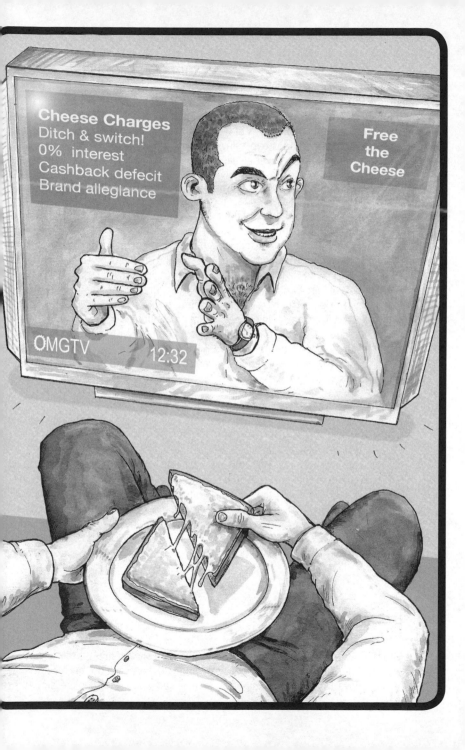

galling for the teenage boy who now wears a jumper with breasts). They make sure that they are photographed around town sporting the latest cheap fashion accessory (paid for of course by some desperate clothing chain that is about to go into liquidation) so that their copycat, airhead followers rush out and do the same. Then of course you find them in the colour supplements of weekend newspapers, sporting a series of joy-inducing poses and wearing cheap shiny, sweatshop-produced dresses and blouses, (which of course they would never actually be seen dead in).

And finally, there is the supremely annoying 'Friend-of-the-Consumer' who is there to protect us silly punters who just aren't saving enough. They foam at the mouth, shouting on television at those who call into the programme having been hoodwinked by loan sharks, or who refuse to dilute their washing up liquid (five parts water to one part washing up liquid if you are interested), or at those who aren't using the supermarket's own brand of mechanically-recovered sausages. This is usually followed by the televisual feast of them poking their nose into the fridges of poor unsuspecting housewives in the early hours of the morning and lambasting them for buying Cathedral City Mature Cheddar instead of some rubbery substitute made from contaminated Chinese milk. They go on and on like some religious zealot ranting about how consumers are making all the wrong financial choices and should be saving money on everything by trading down, not just by one level, but four or five. At the end of the show they can be easily identified, speeding off in their brand new Porsche as they make their way to the up-market delicatessen down the road.

☐ **Tick here when you have spotted the Celebrity Money Saver**

SYMPATHY RATING – 4

For most normal people, the obsession with celebrity has gone too far. Only prepubescent girls and dullards with IQs less than 30 tend to disagree. There is no doubt that we are developing into a society where being an empty-headed celebrity with few valuable skills is the only thing left to aspire to. But what is supremely annoying is the way celebrities line up to tell everyone how much they 'feel our pain' and how, if everyone followed their advice on how to be frugal, everything would be all right. Move over the IMF, the Celebrity Money Saver is here to save the day.

RARITY – 4

Fortunately, not many celebrities have cottoned onto this latest wheeze to steal the limelight as most of them are still too busy looking at their own reflections to even notice that there is a recession. It's just a pity that those who have spotted a gap in the market are given airtime, but I guess we can't do much about that apart from move to Iran where television is state run and celebrities are stoned to death.

WHAT ARE THEY DOING NOW?
Hoping that President Obama and the rest of the G20 can pull the world out of the economic nosedive so that they can go back to wearing Armani and Gucci clothes and driving drunk around the boulevards of California without looking even more out of place than they already are.

AVOIDANCE | REVENGE STRATEGIES
1. Only listen to the advice from those who practice what they preach, which de facto cannot include celebrities.

2. Buy what the hell you like, and if you fancy a nice bowl of caviar or an expensive box of luxury chocolates, go for it. What the heck, you only live once, and have you ever tried own brand foods – they're rubbish.

3. Avoid anything that is associated with celebrities like advertising, endorsements or 'Hello' magazine. They are only doing it because of one or all of the following apply: (a) they need to feed the emptiness they feel; (b) it was the only work available at the time and their agent insisted they take it; or (c) they want to push their latest book or perfume.

4. Set up a price comparison website, called Celebritymoneysaver.com in which you provide money-saving tips on everything from nail clippers to sump oil.

5. Phone-in to one of the television programmes which features a Celebrity Money Saver and pretend to be spending outlandishly on absolutely everything. Watch as they foam at the mouth and have a seizure; it will do their ratings wonders and it might even make watching the programme enjoyable.

THE CELEBRITY MONEY SAVER:

☐ Can blame someone else for their predicament

☐ Only has them self to blame

☐ Deserves our sympathy and should be hugged

☐ Deserves our contempt and should be shot

The Cohabiting Divorcee

During Victorian Times it was perfectly acceptable for a married man to visit prostitutes (I believe both male and female, although the latter was more socially acceptable). In fact, it was believed to be a healthy component to a long and successful marriage. It was a shame that the wife had no such freedom, but at that time she was considered to be the chattel of her husband, so I guess he could do what the hell he liked. Moreover, the notion of divorce was something to be frowned upon, almost as taboo as having illegitimate children or living in the North. Times have changed considerably since then, and thankfully both husbands and wives can visit prostitutes as freely as they like (both male and female, both of which are perfectly acceptable). However, unlike in Victorian Times, when extramarital sex was considered a good thing, these days, people get quite upset by it all and it often ends up in divorce.

There is no doubt that divorce is increasingly easy, you can pretty much go straight to the divorce courts from the church; quickie divorces are all the rage. However, unless you happen to be rich and famous like Madonna or Paul McCartney, who can afford to be taken to the cleaners by their respective spouses, divorce usually means financial suicide for most people, (who usually end up sleeping on the floor of a friend's house or moving from a rather nice four bedroomed house with double garage in a leafy suburb to a one bedroomed flat with noisy neighbours, barking dogs and damp running down the wall). Even the rich and famous try to get their divorce settlements reduced as their vast wealth has taken a bit of a battering in the Credit Crunch.

Before the Credit Crunch happened along, people would be more than happy to divorce and divide up the spoils, which typically meant selling the family home and sharing the massive amounts of equity that had accumulated over the previous decade. In fact, getting your hands on some extra cash was an increasingly popular reason why people were getting unhitched: 'forget infidelity; forget "irreconcilable differences"; just give me the filthy lucre!'. Apart from the occasional crazy incident where the husband would chainsaw the house in half, most things were settled rather messily and much to the delight of the divorce lawyers who would make pots of cash in the process. Since the Credit Crunch, many are saying they have never been busier – lucky them. You can of course make use of the wonders of modern technology and bypass parasitic lawyers by logging onto one of the many online quickie divorce websites. And it is so cheap – £40 to get things going and on top of that they even provide you with a property valuation service too.

It is well known that money problems are one of the root causes of an unsuccessful union and when one partner spends it like water whilst the other is tighter than a gnat's chuff, there are bound to be problems. As people are cast out of their jobs and lifestyles begin to crumble, the divorce rate will undoubtedly rise, it always does in a recession. For most people the credit crunch has meant that although they can get divorced easily and quickly, they actually cannot afford to split up because there is no cash left in the

piggybank (also known as the house) and they can't get a mortgage which is 50 times their individual annual incomes anymore, (sorry, all the reckless banks have been nationalised). So they end up staying in the same house attempting to ignore each other as they go about their daily lives. Such Cohabiting Divorcees, or 'Separated But Living Together' as they are known in the lonely hearts columns, are surprisingly common. They face some interesting problems, including:

- Having to bite their pillows as their new lovers take them to new heights, desperate not to make animal noises and wake the whole family.
- Fending off unwanted offers of group sex sessions from salacious ladies and gentlemen who wander freely around the house, naked from the waist down.
- Trying to find various items which have been hidden by their bitter spouse hell bent on waging psychological warfare.

But every cloud has a silver lining. Because of the reduction in house prices, husbands may be dead keen on selling up as it will at least reduce the payout to their ex-wives. And with the money left over, they can visit as many prostitutes as they damn well like, safe in the knowledge there will be no comeback apart from the odd bout of gonorrhoea.

☐ **Tick here when you have spotted the Cohabiting Divorcee**

SYMPATHY RATING – 9
Divorce is never a pleasant experience, and you have to feel sorry for those who have to continue to live with their former partner even though they clearly hate them. Perhaps they should have been more careful in their selection of husband or wife in the first place, but then hindsight is such a wonderful thing. The good news is that once the recession has ended, they can find new love, marry again and divorce once more, but this time wait until the next boom.

RARITY
As house prices continue to drop and even when they begin to rise again, the numbers of Cohabiting Divorcees will increase as more couples realise that they only married the person they did because they thought they were going to be rich.

WHAT ARE THEY DOING NOW?
Logging onto the millions of lonely hearts sites desperately trying to find someone who (a) they find attractive; (b) has a GSOH; and (c) has a house they can move into.

AVOIDANCE | REVENGE STRATEGIES

1. Only ever marry during a recession, in this way you know your marriage will last at least ten years which is when the next economic collapse is due.

2. Tell them to sell up anyway and split the debt; life is just too short to be living with someone you hate.

3. Suggest they hire a builder to create a plasterboard partition throughout the house so that they can live separate lives. Better still have the house converted into flats and sell one of them to earn some extra money.

4. Set up a cohabiting divorcee house exchange website in which divorcees can swap houses with each other and move in with a divorced partner from another failed union, (rather like 'Ex-Wife Swap'). Who knows, it might end up working to everyone's advantage.

5. Tell them to move back with their parents (assuming they aren't divorced too).

THE COHABITING DIVORCEE:

☐ Can blame someone else for their predicament

☐ Only has them self to blame

☐ Deserves our sympathy and should be hugged

☐ Deserves our contempt and should be shot

The Conspicuous Consumer

According to Aristotle, shopping is the height of human civilization. Now don't get me wrong, Aristotle was a very clever guy but I think he was talking out of his arse when he came up with that gem. Still, it does seem that billions of people have read the philosopher's words of wisdom and taken them to heart. Consumption (not the Victorian variety associated with the slums of the Industrial North and entailing coughing up quantities of lung) has been the order of the day for decades now and especially following the end of the last war when everyone got sick to death of rationing and having to make do with second hand clothes, outside toilets and cooking with lard. We have moved from being a nation of shopkeepers to being a nation of shoppers and with this transformation came the destruction of the village idyll where everyone knew each other and where you could buy all manner of things from the rag and bone man or the quaint old guy who would come by and sharpen all your knives using a contraption on the back of his bicycle. Today we can shop around the clock in huge out of town shopping malls or on the internet, and buy absolutely everything we could ever dream of, never want or indeed ever find a use for. There is no doubt that shopping malls are wondrous things, especially at Christmas time and during the January sales when people come to blows as they fight over the merchandise.

As our traditional hobbies like invading France, street fighting and setting fire to farmers' crops have disappeared along with village life, we have embraced shopping as our major national pastime. And as we became evermore unable to resist the urge to splurge, it wasn't long before shops, aided and abetted by the credit card companies, were doing everything they could to bring conspicuous consumption into all our lives. Showing off with shopping became the best thing in town as women staggered through shops, weighed down by huge bags containing their latest purchases, trying not to topple over on their 15 inch stilettos. With their eyes fixed on the 'must have' Louis Vuitton key ring at the back of the store, they would knock small children and display items flying as they rushed down the aisle with the single mindedness of a Hellfire missile. How they could see, wearing those ridiculously large sunglasses was of course a mystery, but they managed to reach their target anyway. And once they got to the till they could momentarily relax as the shop assistant went carefully through their carbon-footprint-maximising ritual of wrapping it all up. This might take up to 30 minutes and involve a box, tissue paper, a bow, and lots of furtive looks whilst the 'piece de resistance', the ubiquitous oversized bag which could easily accommodate a small Mexican family, is delivered to the customer. As the bulging bag, replete with massive logo (required for advertising), and string handles (required to give the impression it was earth-friendly), was flung over the woman's shoulder, it could take out the eye of any passing shopper.

There was a simple and direct correlation between the number of Conspicuous Consumers and the economic boom: the faster the economy grew, the higher their number. A lesser known fact is that as their numbers grew so did the size of the landfill sites.

The streets would be crammed full of fake fur wearing women with high heels, dark glasses and stupid handbags, as well as fake fur wearing metrosexuals in flip flops and three quarter length slacks. Everyone started to look the same. As did the shops. No matter which town or city you went to, you could be anywhere as the same big named brands cluttered the streets of Britain, competing with bigger and bigger bags. This of course explains why the shopping malls have become so incredibly large, as without the extra space there would be no room to move amongst the clashing bags of the Conspicuous Consumers.

As consumption got out of hand and as the number of Conspicuous Consumers increased, the need to set yourself aside with ever more consumptive behaviour led to more outlandish products being designed to feed the voracious shopper. Not satisfied with any old handbag or item of clothing it had to be exclusive and preferably diamond encrusted. Typical items on the wish list of the Conspicuous Consumer included the £500000 Luvaglio laptop complete with a diamond for the power on button; the £3.5 million diamond encrusted bra from Victoria's Secret; the £7000 diamond encrusted G-String (which could also be used as a bracelet, but only after it had been thoroughly washed first); and not forgetting the £10000 Henk suitcase with its hand-carved Italian walnut interior.

Thankfully with the recession such stupidity if not already over, is well and truly on the way out. New shopping centres remain empty with their backers going bust; expensive brands are going the way of the Dodo, and the Conspicuous Consumers are in hiding from their creditors. If the shops aren't already boarded up they are certainly bereft of shoppers, and teeter on the brink of closure as their parent companies toy with bankruptcy.

As shopping drops down our list of pastimes, it is being replaced by a newfound enthusiasm for street fighting and setting fire to farmers' crops; France is of course no longer worth invading.

☐ **Tick here when you have spotted the Conspicuous Consumer**

SYMPATHY RATING – 1
I could never see the fun in shopping, such a waste of time. But then the whole concept was designed for women, transsexuals and metrosexuals. Normal men rarely went shopping and in any case were only there to carry all the outsized bags. Transaction shopping is far more satisfying and the last thing you need is yet another bloody bag to force into the boot of your car. The poor Conspicuous Consumer drowning in debt and unwanted goods deserves little sympathy.

RARITY – 1
One of the silver linings of the recession is of course that you can now move freely around shopping centres without endangering yourself or

potentially losing a vital organ. You do, however, have to fight through the crowds swarming around the Pound Shops and discount supermarkets.

WHAT ARE THEY DOING NOW?

Being pounced on as they enter the remaining exclusive shops along the high street by desperate salespeople who will do anything and everything to be their friend and secure the only sale of the day. And once they have purchased an item, they now have it passed to them in a small plain bag (rather like the ones you get in sex shops) so that they can continue to spend but in an inconspicuous way.

AVOIDANCE | REVENGE STRATEGIES

1. Move with the times – conspicuous consumption is out and being miserly and tight fisted is in. Rejoice and embrace in the new world of thrift and shopping in Poundland.

2. Demand that VAT is increased to 400% on all diamond encrusted items. Not only will it reduce the trade in very stupid, over priced goods, but it is likely to improve the lives of the poor souls who mine blood diamonds in far flung places like Sierra Leone.

3. As women are now spending their cash on smaller items, such as make-up, to brighten up their otherwise depressing, shopping-free lives, why not open a cheap cosmetics store? As well as stocking lots of pretty make-up, deliver all items to the customers in massive oversized bags so that they can pretend that they have just spent a fortune.

4. Create a Conspicuous Consumption Theme Park on somewhere like the Isle of Capri. Ensure that only high end shops with oversized bags can trade there and only allow people with more money than sense to get in. Keep ten per cent of all the profits.

5. Offer a bag wrapping service to recession conscious Conspicuous Consumers and site yourself in one of the many whitewashed windowed shop units. Wrap all their items in old newspapers and force them into small biodegradable bags which they can pop on the compost heap when they get home.

THE CONSPICUOUS CONSUMER:

☐ Can blame someone else for their predicament

☐ Only has them self to blame

☐ Deserves our sympathy and should be hugged

☐ Deserves our contempt and should be shot

The Credit Crunch Crook

According to the Pope and other church officials, the recession shows us the value of restraint, and a life with less wealth, less sex and more self-imposed discipline (aka self-flagellation) has become more attractive because of the economic downturn. Now this has a lot of merit to it, but the problem is that most people like splashing the cash and having gratuitous amounts of sex is about the only thing you can do right now which isn't taxed, plus it allows you to stop worrying about all the doom and gloom for at least 35 seconds. However, despite all this advice it seems that one cohort in society has chosen to ignore it all – the criminal fraternity.

The primary playground for the Credit Crunch Crook of course has been property. With the screaming middle classes climbing over each other to get hold of anything that contained bricks, they forgot to do the necessary due diligence before joining property investment clubs or signing up for the latest buy-to-let condo development. For the Credit Crunch Crooks, it was like stealing candy from a baby. Buy-to-let scams in which the property-obsessed punter would be told that the houses they were going to invest their life savings in were being refurbished and would always have tenants, have turned to dust.

As well as the classic greed and property related cons, the Credit Crunch Crook focuses on praying upon the worried and newly unemployed. They have developed clever ways to sound genuinely concerned about your plight, whilst stealing everything you have. Typical scams include:

- *The Foreclosure Prevention Specialist* who dupes the desperate householder who is falling behind on their mortgage. Well, when they meant help, what they actually meant was that they would help the worried householder sign over the deeds of the property to them.

- Offering the unemployed *'training schemes'* where their precious redundancy money can be used to pay for valuable training which will see prospective employers clambering over each other to get hold of their hot new skills. Of course, such training is either non-existent, poorly delivered or plain useless and the suckers who get hoodwinked into this are left with no cash, more debt and a sour taste in their mouths. A bit like university students, then.

- Offering *'wealth generating'* seminars where the truly desperate learn how to weather the current storm and even become rich. They offer exclusive information, real nuggets such as 'cash is king' and 'always wash your hands after going to the toilet'. For such pearls of wisdom the muppets who attend will pay £40 and be bullied into paying out a lot more for a personal seminar tailored to their specific needs, like – 'remember to turn off all your appliances at the end of the evening'.

- Running *'Boiler Room'* scams to pressurise would-be investors into buying worthless or bogus shares – typically women and men in their 50s and 60s. Such scams are highly

sophisticated and even include bogus shareholder meetings which the duped investors attend.

Like all criminals, the Credit Crunch Crook will use the money to live it up at the victim's expense buying horses, Inspector Morse's car and lavishing their new found wealth on their inbred families, like some kind of catholic version of Robin Hood.

Of course, it's not just those evil criminals who are dreaming up schemes to replace lost income or get rich off the back of the recessionary misery, it's you and I too, (well, you actually, as I am a law-abiding citizen). For example, the level of insurance related fraud has sky rocketed since the recession started. The usual claims associated with a knocked over vase or a spilled pot of paint worth a few quid at best, have morphed into elaborate accidents which net the fraudster many thousands of Pounds. Typical claims include the guy who had allegedly fallen ill on holiday and paid out loads of cash to aid his recovery when he was actually spending the money on prostitutes, (one can only assume he became ill with all the exertion and required an all over body massage to make him feel better) or the chap who was off sick because of a back injury only to be named player of the year by his local football team.

You see in the end, unless you happen to be a criminal mastermind, you just won't be successful. The general public are mere amateurs where it comes to being a Credit Crunch Crook.

☐ **Tick here when you have spotted the Credit Crunch Crook**

SYMPATHY RATING – 0

Although the old adage, crime doesn't pay sounds good, in reality it is clear that it does. The Credit Crunch Crook is the lowest of the low as they pray on the helpless, the stupid and the insane. So they deserve no sympathy when they are caught. As for the general public who continuously fall for these scams, I find it hard to believe that people still do. I just can't understand it. I mean if some fat geezer drove up to you in Inspector Morse's Jaguar, and offered you the chance of a lifetime wouldn't you be at least a little bit suspicious? I would, but it seems that even accountants who are meant to be good with the money get duped so maybe I am just a cynical old git who trusts no one.

RARITY – 4

Thankfully, in the great scheme of things, the number of Credit Crunch Crooks is still relatively small, although their numbers are growing as the criminal fraternity look for new ways to con people out of their money. They will soon be joined by the increasingly desperate general public pretending to collect for charity and pocketing the whole lot (buttons and all).

WHAT ARE THEY DOING NOW?
Thumbing though the newspapers to find the latest announcement of massive job losses and then ringing up the poor souls who have lost their jobs to offer them a range of options to retrain. Or re-launching new property companies (after their old one collapsed) focussing on distressed sellers. Undeterred, the Credit Crunch Crooks relentlessly look for ways to fleece the unsuspecting public and bolster their cash flow.

AVOIDANCE | REVENGE STRATEGIES
1. Remember the old adage, 'shame on you, if you fool me once; shame on me if you fool me twice'.

2. If you happen to have some cash either because you have been made redundant, come into an inheritance or because you have been saving diligently for years, hold onto it. There is no point in wasting it on some bogus training scam or hoping to make massive returns through property (haven't you learned your lesson yet?). You are better off using it to eat or buy a few more copies of this excellent book.

3. Steer clear of any odd sounding company which purports to be there to help you, like 'Lovely Dream Homes', 'Parrott's Paradise Properties', or 'Fly-by-night Training' and of course keep well away from absolutely anything that has been endorsed by celebrities.

4. Set-up a mobile Credit Crunch Crook Advice Unit which goes around the country offering the young, old and newly unemployed advice on avoiding being taken for a ride. Ideally your vehicle of choice should be an ambulance as this will present a friendly and familiar sight to those using your service. Seek some government grants to get you going and consider having a picture of Gordon Brown on the sides – the arch Credit Crunch Crook!

5. Set up a Credit Crunch Crook finishing school in which Credit Crunch Crooks are offered a safe and non-judgemental learning environment in which to test out new ideas to fleece people. Offer full board and en-suite bathrooms as well as video links to the jail cells of well-known crooks.

THE CREDIT CRUNCH CROOK:

☐ Can blame someone else for their predicament

☐ Only has them self to blame

☐ Deserves our sympathy and should be hugged

☐ Deserves our contempt and should be shot

The Credit Crunch Scrounger

There has always been a cohort in society who for whatever reason has felt compelled to scrounge off other people. Before we dismiss them it is important to take into account the recent theories put forward by anthropologists who believe this behaviour is a throwback to prehistoric times. Apparently, being able to scrounge was one of the principal skills required to survive in the competitive environment of the cave and the dangerous and usually life-threatening surroundings outside. For example, borrowing your fellow Neanderthal's spear often meant that he was killed rather than you, and scrounging a bit of sex off one of the hirsute women of the tribe was a sure fire way to make it to the top of the tree. The same anthropologists also believe that there is a scrounging gene and are currently working with the Human Genome Project to continue their research and isolate it.

Although many of us may scrounge from time to time, (you know, like borrowing a cup of sugar when you have moved house or using a friend's spare room after you have found your husband in bed with another man), most of us do not adopt this as a lifestyle choice. However, there are plenty of people that do and have no compunction in continuing to scrounge off anyone they can and especially the state. These are the people who never seem to have anything; no money, no fags, no food, nowhere to stay and of course, no friends. They are always happy for you or me to buy them beer all night, but when it comes to their round, they seem to be in a tearing hurry to go home to their sick mother. And whenever you need them to pay up for something, they will always claim to be fresh out of cash, or to have forgotten their wallet. Although you may mistake them for being Scottish, they are in fact professional scroungers. And now that the recession is in full swing they have got the perfect excuse to take their art form to a new level and push the 'scrounging envelope' even further, so to speak. Typical Credit Crunch Scrounger strategies include:

- *The 'I'm fresh out of cash and need a train fare home' routine.* This is a classic ploy that usually takes place nowhere near a train station. As you are standing in the street admiring the architecture or perhaps a beautiful lady who is walking past, they mosey up to you and before you can push them in front of an oncoming cyclist, they start telling you their tale of woe and how because of this and that and the Credit Crunch they haven't got their train fare home. They claim only to want a few pounds, which we all know is useless these days, unless you've purchased a 'Super Saver Ticket'. Up to this point you may have been considering giving them the cash just so that they bugger off and leave you alone. Only they blow it by offering to pay it back – yeah, like when and how? When you tell them that you can't spare them any money – after

all there is a recession on right now – they hurl abuse at you and storm off before regaining their composure ready for their next target.

- The *'Can you lend me a fag?' con*. Similar to the above, this is another attempt by a perfect stranger to get something for nothing. As they walk up the road, usually near pubs, they spot a smoker and try to get a cigarette off of them without paying anything. And if they are unsuccessful they ask the next person and so on until they secure a smoke.

- The *'Can you lend some cash so that I can buy you a drink?' classic*. This is mainly perpetrated by students who given the parlous state of the education system have to resort to borrowing money from their friends so that they can buy a pint. In such instances I would strongly recommend that they brew their own as it will be cheaper and the alcoholic content will be significantly greater than the crap sold in the Student Union bar.

In addition to the classic 'something for nothing' techniques, there are a couple which are particularly suited to life in the Credit Crunch:

- The *'Living it big on state benefits' bonanza*. This one is favoured by large families who can no longer be bothered to work; in fact they make so much money from state benefits that they actually never have to work again. Although they have absolutely everything paid for them they complain that the Credit Crunch is costing them dear and they need even more state handouts, despite spending £3000 on Christmas presents for their ever growing family. And when challenged on why they haven't worked for 23 years they cite irritable bowel syndrome as the reason.

- The *'Can I live in the boot of your car, or perhaps your garden shed?' request*. This is a relatively new one and shows the ingenuity of the Credit Crunch Scrounger. Having lost their house they will ask if they can live, albeit temporarily, in the boot of your car and assume that if you have two cars it will serve as a two bedroomed apartment. Those who have sheds at their allotments tend to be pestered at weekends when groups of scroungers enquire if they can use the shed as a hostel until they sort themselves out. Unfortunately, in many cases, they already have a family of eight living in them and reluctantly they have to move on.

☐ **Tick here when you have spotted the Credit Crunch Scrounger**

SYMPATHY RATING – **5**

How much sympathy the Credit Crunch Scrounger deserves depends on *(a)* how often they scrounge; *(b)* what they are scrounging; *(c)* how long they have been scrounging for; and *(d)* who they scrounge off. Clearly the state is happy to let anyone scrounge and with all the extra cash that is being printed, there should be more than enough to go around.

RARITY - 6

You'd be surprised at the number of Credit Crunch Scroungers, and their numbers are set to increase over the next seven or eight years which the recession is expected to run. If it's anything like America, then it won't be long before over 50% of the country will be living in other people's cars and this will no doubt spawn a new car-to-let bubble which will only end in tears.

WHAT ARE THEY DOING NOW?

Developing new and advanced methods of scrounging using a range of hypnosis, auto suggestion and neuro linguistic programming techniques which have been developed and fine-tuned by magicians and con artists.

AVOIDANCE | REVENGE STRATEGIES

1. Although you might be tempted to scrounge the occasional thing off someone you know or indeed a complete stranger, it is generally better not to unless you intend to return the favour. If most people are like me, it will be a one time only affair and next time you will be liable for a smack in the teeth.

2. Write the definitive guide to scrounging in which you provide the amateur scrounger with an A-Z guide on the tricks of the trade.

3. Why not investigate how much you could get from the state and compare this with what you earn. If the state pays more I would suggest that you join all the other scroungers, and I am not just talking about those who work in government.

4. Outlaw any form of scrounging and make it a capital offence.

5. Introduce a Scrounger Card which allows scroungers to monitor the number of times they have successfully scrounged something. Operating in the same way as a customer loyalty scheme, after ten scrounges you get a free gift, like an extra fag or pint of beer. Sell them for a small fee to scroungers and provide a list of valuable free gifts. Don't forget to provide an ink stamp which has an outstretched hand as its symbol.

THE CREDIT CRUNCH SCROUNGER:

☐ Can blame someone else for their predicament

☐ Only has them self to blame

☐ Deserves our sympathy and should be hugged

☐ Deserves our contempt and should be shot

The Deadbeat Debtor

Over the last decade or so, our relationship with debt has somehow completely morphed. Once, going into debt was a shameful necessity which was occasionally required. Now it's something to be embraced, enjoyed, maximised even. And like most things that have been imported from the good old US of A, (like political correctness, obesity and Taco Bell), the notion that debt was good soon took off. Off we went, piling it up as though it was free money that never needed to be paid back. Apart from the government and businesses that couldn't get enough of the stuff, it was the consumer that really decided to go crazy and spend, spend, spend. Fuelled by programmes and advertisements that piped the lifestyles of the rich and famous into the living rooms of the nation, people were no longer willing to save up for that special holiday, the new car or leopard skin trouser suit. Instead all they needed was a few dozen credit cards, loans and equity release schemes to fill their pockets with excess cash. As the adverts would suggest, why wait when you can have it now?

What they meant of course is that you can have the debt now. Over the last few years people have been lining-up at shop counters to sign up for the latest store card so that they could save £1.50 when they spent £4500 on clothes, or they've used their homes as cash point machines to maintain the lavish lifestyles so convincingly portrayed in 'Eastenders' and 'Emmerdale'. And although they might have occasionally worried about how much money they owed, it was easy to get around the problem by signing up for yet another credit card, collecting them in the same way that teenage kids pick up sexually transmitted diseases. At that time opening up your wallet or purse to display a myriad of bronze, silver, gold, platinum and black cards was cool and one of the best ways to make new friends or attract muggers. Then the credit card companies decided to allow you to design you own card with cheesy pictures of your grandma taking her last breath in the emphysema clinic so that it would somehow make racking up a shed load of debt a more personal and rewarding experience. As you see her face pass through the card swipe and enter your pin you momentarily look back on her long and happy life and remember that you had forgotten to buy some fags.

Then it all came to a grinding halt with the Credit Crunch. All of a sudden the banks and loan companies realised that they had been a bit silly. The number of Deadbeat Debtors became unmanageable and as they fell behind on their loan and credit card repayments at an alarming rate, they started to impact profits. So what did they do? They cut people's credit lines, sold the bad debts to violent debt collectors and all of a sudden developed a conscience. And the poor old Deadbeat Debtor – well, they were well and truly stuffed. Of course in the past, debt and in particular debtors were frowned upon, especially if you happened to be poor. Naturally, kings and queens could borrow massive amounts of cash from Italian banks to wage war with their neighbours and buy gold braided pantaloons and then default causing the bank to go bust. They could do this because they were second only to God. Those who weren't kings or

queens, or curried favour with them, tended to find themselves in debtor's prison which was a rather unsavoury place to be. Unfortunately we don't have debtor's prisons anymore, which is just as well because nearly the whole population would be inside right now.

Never one to miss an opportunity, loan sharks and dodgy banks you have never heard of, like 'Lose Your Shirt Bank Plc', have spent millions advertising to the Deadbeat Debtors convincing them that debt is okay and they can make everything better if they transfer all their debts to them. They always show a worried middle aged couple surrounded by piles of unopened shopping bags poring over their bills looking confused by the size and scale of their debts and wondering how they'll ever pay it all back. Then, having consolidated all their debts into 'one single easy monthly payment' the sun shines and there are smiles all round as they resume their reckless spending, comfortable in the knowledge that the one easy payment will take them well and truly over the edge.

☐ **Tick here when you have spotted the Deadbeat Debtor**

SYMPATHY RATING – **2**
Anyone who spent way beyond their means deserves little or no sympathy, after all it is their own fault and they can't complain that the nasty loan or credit card company forced them to spend money they hadn't got. Had they only listened to the simple arithmetic classes at school that explained how three apples could be shared out between Johnny, Ginny and Timmy then they may not have found themselves in the pickle they do now.

RARITY – **10**
The numbers in debt started off quite small and tended to be restricted to those who over extended themselves with their mortgages. Since then the Deadbeat Debtors' ranks have swelled as the maxed out mortgagees have been joined by the car loan losers and the credit card collectors, all massively in debt with nowhere to go but the bankruptcy court.

WHAT ARE THEY DOING NOW?
Starring in television programmes like 'All Maxed Out' where they are lectured on the need to live within their means and shown how to pay off the £250000 worth of debt they managed to accumulate over the course of 14 months whilst on a salary of £12500. Those unlucky enough not to be able to wash their dirty laundry in public queue patently outside the Citizens Advice Bureau to hear that there is no help available to them and that they should go home and await the sound of their front door being smashed in by the debt collector.

AVOIDANCE | REVENGE STRATEGIES

1. When given the choice as to whether to spend or save, always save first. Then, when everyone else is mired in debt and the shops are desperate to sell, you will be able to pick up some excellent bargains.

2. Understand how bad debt can be when it gets out of hand. If you do need to borrow money, do it wisely, unless of course you don't give a toss and are more than happy to spend recklessly and then go bankrupt.

3. Give the Deadbeat Debtor a copy of that wonderful Shakespearean tome – 'The Merchant of Venice'. If they don't understand the important message the play contains they will at least be put into a coma by the mind numbingly boring and incomprehensible drivel contained between its covers.

4. Set up a modern day debtor's prison in which the heavily indebted can quite literally work off their debt. In these ecological times, I would recommend that you build massive treadmills linked to dynamos for the indebted inmates to walk on for 10 hours at a time. The 'green' energy produced can be linked directly to the national grid and the money they generate from selling the electricity (I think in the order of two pence per Kilowatt per hour) can be used to pay off their debt. With the average owed being around £30000 it will only take approximately 411 years to clear it.

5. Launch a new television campaign aimed at the Deadbeat Debtors called Debt4U in which you consolidate their debts and charge them a highly competitive 850% interest rate (which will save them money when compared to all the store cards they have). Ideally this should be fronted by a has-been celebrity, game show host or ex-soap star who needs the cash and who can look serious and make strange gestures with their hands. Ensure that you include lots of pictures of fast cars, scantily clad women and the odd testimonial of a married couple mired in debt.

THE DEADBEAT DEBTOR:

☐ Can blame someone else for their predicament

☐ Only has them self to blame

☐ Deserves our sympathy and should be hugged

☐ Deserves our contempt and should be shot

The Desperate Estate Agent

I believe that anyone who has a job that has the word 'agent' in it isn't worthy of much respect. Acting as they do as middlemen between the sellers and buyers of products and services seems to be so outdated in today's technology driven world. Technology aside, the other thing about those who profess to be agents is that they can put in the minimum of amount of effort and still expect you to pay them their cut. But even worse than that is when you ring them up to catch up on progress (i.e. to see if they have actually done any work on your behalf), they always seem to be focused on your deal at that precise moment and usually tell you that they are just about to send your CV/proposal/house details to a potential client. This of course is a complete lie which they say to everyone that rings. You see, unless the agent sees you as a massive cash cow they can't be arsed and would rather wait for you to kick them up the butt than be proactive. Although all kinds of agent, apart from perhaps secret agents (at least they kill the enemies of the state), are useless, there is one that has always set themselves aside from the others, and that's the estate agent. For a long time, the career of choice of any low achieving school leaver who never quite knew what they wanted to do in life, being an estate agent was easy – sit around in an office for most of the day; wait until someone rings you up to sell their house; take a few details; visit said house; make a few qualitative statements, like 'this is bit 1970s'; take a few measurements; take a photo; put up a board; print off a few flyers; add it to the website and … er that's it apart from handing the details to a buyer, showing them around and then making a pathetic attempt at negotiating a deal. In total about 47 minutes work for a 1–3% commission; you just can't beat it.

As the housing boom continued it was like taking candy from a baby and they even did their best to maximise their commission by goading would-be buyers to 'gazump' on properties where the sale was already agreed. This didn't exactly endear them to the original buyers, mind you I am sure the sellers loved it. It wasn't long before you'd see estate agents driving around in gaudy Minis, happy in the knowledge that they would be making a six figure sum for doing next to nothing. At the top end of the market it was even easier, as rich tycoons from across the world would flock to cities such as London to buy absolutely anything that was grotesquely expensive so that they could show off to the other billionaires. Property envy was all the rage and the estate agents were beside themselves with joy.

Since the property boom turned rapidly into bust, the estate agent has almost been made extinct and those that are left have become increasingly desperate as they finally realise they may actually have to work for a living. As the market tumbles by double digit percentages, they play the glad game as they try to convince would-be buyers that the market has bottomed out and now is the time to get back into property. They also latch onto any trend in a vain attempt to influence property prices. For example, as the middle classes have embraced the need to feed themselves economically by ploughing

up their beautifully manicured lawns and growing stuff, estate agents are suggesting that a well tended vegetable garden can add thousands to the asking price of a property, and can also 'widen the market' for your home. Typical estate agent bunkum. I guess if you were very lucky you might get a couple of farmers interested.

Never one to miss the chance to move at least one property a month, the Desperate Estate Agent will also come up with sales gimmicks such as 'buy a house, get a free divorce'. Admittedly this has become common in Spain which is even more of a basket case than the UK – with over one million properties lying empty, Spanish estate agents are even more desperate than ours. The deal is simple, if you happen to be living with some bastard or bitch you don't love anymore, then the agency will give you free access to their lawyers, (who can clearly do more than just conveyancing, clever fellows), to sort out your divorce so long as you buy a new house from them. One assumes that the person on the losing side gets the crappiest house. The same agency also does a deal for those contemplating marriage with an 'all expenses paid' wedding when you buy one of their properties. It's great, you can divorce and remarry and get your housing needs addressed at the same time.

Of course the poor old estate agent has yet to grasp the fundamental economics of supply and demand, and also gravity, (what goes up must come down). With the credit markets seized up and the UK fast becoming the land of the taxed-to-death, no one in their right mind will be buying a new house anytime soon. Even the rich tycoons have recognised that the country has gone to the dogs and are busy buying houses in the new global property hotspot – Kabul. Apparently the Taliban do a great deal on two bedroomed apartments.

☐ **Tick here when you have spotted the Desperate Estate Agent**

*SYMPATHY RATING – **1***
It really is very difficult to be sympathetic to the estate agent's plight and in many respects they can be blamed for bigging up the housing market over the last ten years. Always one to make a quick buck, they would operate with the integrity of a Gravy Train Politician and push up the asking price of even the most grottiest of semis. And now that it's all gone tits up, they expect some sympathy – jog on!

*RARITY – **10***
Although some 50000 estate agents may end up losing their jobs (I can see your tears from here), those that remain are beyond desperate. Their cheesy enthusiasm is matched only by the beads of sweat rolling down their forehead as they clock you walking through their door. They look and behave like a Jehovah's Witness who has been invited into someone's house.

WHAT ARE THEY DOING NOW?
Still working on the latest wheeze to convince buyers that's its okay to accept a 25% reduction in their asking price, and in order to sweeten the deal, they'll have sex with one or both of the sellers. Apparently this works like a dream.

AVOIDANCE | REVENGE STRATEGIES
1. Always remember that your house is a home first and an investment second. Get used to the fact that you won't be able to use your house as (a) a piggybank, or (b) as your pension.

2. Always aim to sell your property yourself by using one of the many property websites. Better still, make you own For Sale board and march up and down your local area with it strapped to your back.

3. Steer clear of property until the UK becomes a business and tax friendly country; be prepared to wait a very, very, long time.

4. Write to a television producer with an exciting new reality TV programme called '*Estate Agents do the stupidest of things (to sell a house)*'. Have Desperate Estate Agents send in hilarious video clips of them dressing up as the Pope in order to sell a convent which has been converted into luxury flats.

5. Establish your own estate agency and offer your clients a funeral service with every house they purchase. If there is no one who is about to croak it, offer a contract killing service instead where the killer will liquidate someone of the buyer's choice.

THE DESPERATE ESTATE AGENT:

☐ Can blame someone else for their predicament

☐ Only has them self to blame

☐ Deserves our sympathy and should be hugged

☐ Deserves our contempt and should be shot

The Disposed of Worker (previously known as Our Most Important Asset)

L ong before the Black Death and the Peasants' Revolt in 1381, when workers finally began to flex their economic muscles, the average employee (or serf as they were technically known at that time) was treated like dirt by the Lord of the Manor. They laboured long hours, under appalling conditions and in all weathers just so the lord could live it up in his fancy mansion holding extravagant banquets for his regal friends and wearing outsized codpieces. What little produce was left over, such as the occasional potato, had to feed a growing family of ten. But to top it all, whenever there was a battle to fight, the poor old peasant had to go armed with his pitchfork. Unfortunately for him this was often no match for a knight on horseback wielding a very long lance and very sharp sword and he often wound up in pieces scattered about the battlefield. Since the Black Death and the Peasants' Revolt however, things have steadily improved. Workers no longer have to toil under terrible conditions (well apart from those in the sweatshops of Asia), they no longer have to go and fight with farm implements, these days it is with balance sheets and teams of corporate lawyers. In fact, things aren't half bad all things considered. However, the Lord of the Manor has been replaced by the chief executive who likes to live it up in their fancy mansion, throwing wild parties for their political friends and wearing expensive silk slacks.

Achieving this improvement has been comparatively simple and largely the result of an illusion created by academics, HR and chief executives that the workers were the company's most important asset and that those who ran the company actually cared about them. This illusion was fuelled by gimmicks such as 'Employee of the Month' – where an unsuspecting and typically lowly-paid employee would be given a plastic badge with 'You're Special' or some other suitably patronising phrase emblazoned on it. Feeling like they had just won the lottery their motivation levels would increase and their boss would get a few extra hours work out of them for free. The few pence spent on the badge seemed to do the trick and employees lapped up the propaganda, much to the joy of the chief executive and of course our friends in HR; much cheaper than a pay rise. It wasn't long before the plastic badge was joined by an 'Employee of the Month' hall of fame from which the cheesy grins of those selected for special treatment beamed and staff did whatever they could to win the coveted title, including bare knuckle fighting in the canteen. In some instances staff could be treated like dirt for a whole year and then find a metal plaque on their desk telling them how much they were valued. It's amazing how the memory of the bitch that treated them worse than

There There Today
Monday 16th
8.45 AM
Employee of the Month
HMRC
SACKED! (never mind, eh)
Still to come... TV's Z-list beach bodies on a budget!

a concentration camp prison guard was completely erased! Other techniques to show that they cared included the company magazine and motivational posters showing irrelevant pictures of snow covered mountains and trite phrases about teamwork, success, risk and lavatorial etiquette.

The 'you're our most important asset' mantra always reaches a crescendo when employment markets are tight, or when the organisation is desperate to hold onto those people who actually turn up and do some work every day. But when times get tough, well we all know what happens. It all goes rather quiet as staff are kicked out of their jobs and HR (as always) fails to add any value at all. The cheese stops and HR no longer bothers to show any concern; no more badges, no more special awards ceremonies, it's now a case of 'you're lucky to have a job, so stop whining and get back to work'. And like puppy dogs desperate to please, the workers go back to their desks and put in even more hours, (for no extra pay, and more than likely less, following pay cuts).

Many dedicated people who gave their body and soul to the company can't quite believe what is happening to them when they lose their job. If you are careful you can see them walking out of their offices in a state of shock with tears running down their cheeks, struggling with cardboard boxes which contain the sum total of their career, no doubt thinking to themselves, 'so, is that it?' Meanwhile, their colleagues are delighted that the arsehole from Accounts or the moron from Marketing has finally gone; you should always remember that companies rarely get rid of their best staff.

In the end you have to recognise that all of us are expendable, mere economic refugees washed up on the shores of an unsuspecting employer; just resources to be used as required, rather like items of stationary (although arguably less useful). And like the donkey that is no longer of use to its owner, it's off to the Knacker's yard to be quietly dispatched and cut up for value beef burgers.

☐ **Tick here when you have spotted the Disposed of Worker (previously known as Our Most Important Asset)**

 SYMPATHY RATING – 9
Unlike so many people affected by the recession, the Disposed of Worker (previously known as Our Most Important Asset) is worthy of our sympathy. It is a grim business to be told you are surplus to requirements, especially after having worked at the same place for most of your natural life. However, I struggle to believe that so many people are taken in by the superficial crap about how important they are to the companies they work for. HR is clearly doing a grand job and maybe they should be renamed the Human Delusion Department.

 RARITY – 7
With unemployment reaching record levels the numbers of Disposed of Workers (previously known as Our Most Important Asset) will no doubt

increase. And no matter how many slogans the government come up with, such as 'British jobs for British workers' things won't be changing anytime soon.

WHAT ARE THEY DOING NOW?

Appearing on cheesy morning chat shows presented by grossly overpaid patronising interviewers who feign genuine concern and say things like 'Ooooh I know how bad it can be' and 'I think you'd be a really, really, really really, really, good teacher, you will inspire a generation'. For God's sake spare us! If they can't find their way onto television, they will be queuing up with the rest of the unemployed at the local job centre.

AVOIDANCE | REVENGE STRATEGIES

1. Recommend they go into freelancing as this will allow them to recover their self esteem, make more money, and more importantly, free themselves from all those goddamn plastic badges and motivational bullshit.

2. Pretend you have been kicked out of your job too to show solidarity with them and join them in a rant about how evil all employers are and how they don't care about their staff.

3. Give them a small parcel of books to read, including 'Das Capital' by Karl Marx, 'The Disposable American' by Louis Uchitelle and 'Ethics, Integrity and Sacrifice in the Workplace' by Clarke Westerne of Despair.com. These will help them understand their true role in the workplace.

4. Prepare a newspaper supplement – 'The Top 100 Best Companies for Casting Out Their Employees with Little or no Payout' and distribute it through the Sunday newspapers.

5. Offer a boss-napping service in which you snatch bastard bosses who have made their staff redundant. Take them to a disused warehouse and chain them up. Once the crying has stopped bring in the newly disposed of staff and start negotiating with the boss to reinstate them.

THE DISPOSED OF WORKER (PREVIOUSLY KNOWN AS OUR MOST IMPORTANT ASSET):

☐ Can blame someone else for their predicament

☐ Only has them self to blame

☐ Deserves our sympathy and should be hugged

☐ Deserves our contempt and should be shot

The Downwardly Mobile

Wherever you find a socialist government you will always find an obsession with upward mobility and social reengineering, but there is nowhere quite as fanatical about it all as the UK, where it is enshrined in government policy. In a country so preoccupied with class it is no wonder that left wingers love the opportunity to take a street urchin from the backstreets of Birmingham and propel them into the realms of the highly educated ranks of the professional classes. It proves to everyone than anyone can make it and that living in some grimy bedsit on the edge of a disused tin mine should be no barrier to upward mobility. In fact, according to many socialists, it is the ideal breeding ground for the country's future captains of industry. Naturally, the only reason why the left wingers are so into upward mobility is that it gives them more people to tax to death. And although the United States tries to mimic the UK's success, they always end up failing because all they can tell people is to live the American Dream, which usually means getting into the country illegally and driving substandard yellow cabs in New York. Plus all that people need in America to be socially mobile is a credit card with a $30000 limit.

For a time the policies seemed to work because the old toffee-nosed, inbred, public school educated generals of industry were being replaced by the slightly dishevelled unhygienic thugs from rundown council estates. The fact that anyone from a decent background was being penalised as part of the social experiment and as a result was no longer allowed to attend good universities had nothing to do with it of course. You would see Labour politicians and their curly haired socialist chums interviewed in the press regaling the journalist with stories about how boys who used to urinate through old peoples' letterboxes had made it into Oxford to read Classics and were, as a result, destined for great things in their lives.

Things are different now. And as Newton clearly demonstrated when he threw a sharp knife into the air in one of the quadrangles at Cambridge University; what goes up, must come down. Today upward mobility has been replaced by downward mobility and plenty of it. For many, things are looking dire as bankers become teachers, teachers become shop assistants, shop assistants become toilet cleaners and toilet cleaners well just end up in the shit. And this time around we don't hear much from the meddling socialists because everyone has realised that they were talking rubbish and that in the end it has nothing to with class and everything to do with simple economics. And as they see their careers ebb away they are desperately formulating new theories on downward mobility and how this is great news for the economy. Still, we should count ourselves very lucky as we have an incredibly generous government who is going to use all of it's tax-raising powers to accelerate downward mobility and finally bring in the much vaunted classless Britain.

However, it is only when we compare ourselves to other countries that we can truly understand what downward mobility means in practice. For example:

- In the United States the American Dream is turning out to be the American Nightmare in which those who believed that anything was possible didn't realise it actually meant anything remotely resembling failure. With millions losing their jobs, the Downwardly Mobile are massing in tented cities in California just like they did during the Great Depression. The people who live in them, known as campers, come from all walks of life, but mainly the professional classes; former bankers, accountants, financial advisors, mortgage brokers and wrinkled, used-up porn stars who can no longer make it even in the granny-sex genre of the industry. Pictures of toothless women wearing dungarees shooting the breeze with men sporting ill-fitting slacks and discarded clown's boots adorn the newspapers with headlines such as 'where did he get those boots?'

- In Japan they are sending the Downwardly Mobile to state funded programmes where they can learn the lost art of medieval farming. Recently unemployed software engineers and teachers compete against each other for coveted slots in which the 50 lucky winners get to live in cramped conditions without running water or a flushable toilet and spend hours picking up chicken poo to reuse as fertilizer, or weeding 1000 acre fields before planting them with Satsumaimo potatoes. And those fortunate enough not to be selected they can always become homeless – the ultimate in downward mobility. However, they had better be on their best behaviour because Japanese tramps are well behaved, clean and don't like newcomers encroaching on their turf. Unlike in the UK where you would be glassed and left for dead, in Japan they have published rules and a code of conduct that would put any banking CEO to shame and are a dab hand with a samurai sword.

- In China they are buried alive.

☐ **Tick here when you have spotted the Downwardly Mobile**

SYMPATHY RATING – **9**
Although we may read about the ranks of the unemployed, the Downwardly Mobile are the silent victims of the Credit Crunch and recession. Their dreams in tatters, the once ambitious astrophysicist or highly talented forensic accountant can be seen dreaming away as they ask you whether you want fries with that. As they say, recessions are a great leveller. Naturally, no sympathy whatsoever for downwardly mobile politicians; they deserve everything they get.

RARITY – **8**
As the recession grinds on and whole categories of jobs are eliminated from the economy the downwardly mobile are simple to spot. The best place to see them is in car showrooms where they are trading down their silver Mercedes for brown Skodas and at job centres where they are taking advice on how to hide decades of experience and their bucket loads of qualifications in order to reach the shortlist for a Pizza Delivery Boy position that's just come available.

WHAT ARE THEY DOING NOW?
Figuring out how to fit all their worldly possessions and family of five into a three man tent which they bought at a car boot sale and seeing if the clown's boots which they also picked up go well with their pin stripe suit.

AVOIDANCE | REVENGE STRATEGIES
1. If you find yourself on the path of downward mobility, tell everyone that you are about to go on a long assignment and may not be around for a couple of years.

2. Cash-in on the zeitgeist by launching a new family board game called 'Downwardly Mobile' in which you follow the career paths of those impacted by the recession. As the players move around the board they will be subjected to random economic events, such as redundancy or bankruptcy. Make it more interesting by introducing Share the Tents cards and Job-opportunity Knocks cards. When there is nothing else to do during the long summer evenings, it will be a lot of fun; poignant too.

3. Create a new charity which is designed to raise awareness about downward mobility. Consider having your slogan as 'Kissing goodbye to downward mobility' and have a logo of a boy being kicked over a rugby post by a suited gentleman wearing size 10 steel toe capped boots.

4. Remake that film classic 'Trading Places' by bringing it up to the 21st century. Instead of taking a poor guy off the streets, take a young professional from a law firm. Ensure he gets into all sorts of scrapes at the local dump and see if Eddie Murphy will take the lead role.

5. Set yourself up as advisor to the downwardly mobile. Offer advice on how to lie on your CV, how to erect tents and what types of clown outfits are best for different skin tones.

THE DOWNWARDLY MOBILE:

☐ Can blame someone else for their predicament

☐ Only has them self to blame

☐ Deserves our sympathy and should be hugged

☐ Deserves our contempt and should be shot

The Dubai Deserter

I can't see the fascination with Dubai, nothing but sun, sea, sand and, er, shopping – sex is generally out of the question, especially if you fancy a bit of slap and tickle in public, like on the beach. That kind of thing lands you in jail and once you have been flogged in public and completed your 200 year prison term in an airless cell, you are generally deported (which in many respects is the best thing that could happen to you – if only they'd done that in the first place). Since Dubai ran out of oil, it has transformed itself into the playground for the rich, famous and money-grabbing expats which explains why the place is so vacuous, soulless and packed with posers and hangers-on. Just one of the reasons why it's not worth visiting.

Over the years I have had to endure a succession of wannabe expats telling me how great it is in Dubai: the shopping is amazing; the 20 star hotels are well worth the crazy prices; you get to see stars like David Beckham; and the sand is lovely when you can actually stand on it, (which is usually eleven o'clock at night). On and on they go like one of the great bores of today; the kind of person to avoid at barbecues. One guy was like a broken record – every time I bumped into him in the office he would foam at the mouth, his spit rolling down my computer screen as he insisted that I invest in The Palm as 'it is an amaaaaaazing place'. He had at least two properties out there and they would make him piles of cash. Well, one assumes not right now. With prices dropping faster than a tart's knickers the self-proclaimed 'Eighth Wonder of the World' is rapidly turning out to be the first blunder of the world. Dredged from the seabed of the Persian Gulf (or was it the sewers), at a cost of $12 billion, The Palm propelled Dubai into the ranks of the world's most desirable locations. And now with its beaches littered with toilet roll and human faeces (which I am sure I didn't see in the brochures) and after a few more years of global warming, The Palm will be transformed into a mere frond with all the rich and famous washed away into the Gulf, dodging the turds as they swim for their lives.

Not to be left behind as the boom took hold, thousands of Brits flocked to Dubai to get a piece of the action (in fact over three and half million of them), either taking out loans to buy luxury properties they couldn't afford or working on the gazillion building developments, earning more in ten minutes than they did in a month flipping burgers back home; all tax free which is of course the only reason why anyone would be willing to go out there. Life was good; fast cars, shopping and the occasional bit of sex in public (but only when the sand was cool enough). The only issues they had to deal with were the other expats, the intense heat (which means you spend most of the time indoors, shopping mainly), and the constant noise and dust from building work that could only take place in the dead of night. What could possibly go wrong?

As the Credit Crunch progressed and as Dubai rapidly went down the toilet both meta-phorically and physically, the fatheaded idiots who once waxed lyrical about the wonderful lifestyle and the year-round sun tan have been coming home in their droves as

companies go bust, building work is suspended and businesses pull out of the country. The Dubai Deserter's lot wouldn't be so bad if they hadn't been seduced by the celeb lifestyle, (too much time spent watching lifestyle shows and shopping I'm afraid), and spent way beyond their means. The problem they face is that under Sharia law if they can't repay their debts, they tend to find themselves in jail along with all the people caught having sex in public. Sounds like a really free and easy place Dubai, where clearly nothing goes. So what does the Dubai Deserter do? What any law abiding citizen would do; scarper. Faced with crippling debts as a result of their high living, the Dubai Deserter drives to the airport in their soft-top Mercedes, parks up the car, leaves their maxed-out credit cards on the front seat along with the keys to their Dubai Marina apartment, and gets onto the first flight back home. It is far better to swap a lengthy jail sentence for some bedsit in Scunthorpe than take your chances with the police. The only problem of course is that they can never return; mind you, who would go there in the first place?

☐ **Tick here when you have spotted the Dubai Deserter,**

SYMPATHY RATING – 2
It is difficult to feel sorry for the Dubai Deserter given that they were exceptionally annoying even before they went, and they are possibly even more excruciating now that they are back. They spend hours bemoaning the loss of lifestyle, the lack of sun, the fact that they had to leave their Porsche at the airport. As they nurse a drink in their local pub, they gather in groups rather like lepers, complaining about the state of the economy, how expensive everything is and bitching that they have to pay taxes: welcome to the real world. And to cap it all, even their tans begin to fade; Scunthorpe here they come.

RARITY – 6
The Dubai Deserter is surprisingly common, you can normally spot them by their incredible all over tan (yes even under their underpants and knickers) and their flip-flops; it seems that they can't seem to accept that these are not an acceptable form of footwear for the office. With 1500 visas being cancelled every day and as the overloaded-with-debt-expats swarm back to the UK, you should expect to see plenty of them at the Job Centres, looking for opportunities for which they are eminently suited; debt counsellors.

WHAT ARE THEY DOING NOW?
Living in a cold damp bedsit thumbing through the job adverts in the local newspaper. In between worrying about how they will now make ends meet, they will look longingly at Google Earth zeroing in on the Palm desperately trying to locate their two-bedroomed apartment which is now lying dormant and whose toilet is no doubt blocked.

AVOIDANCE | REVENGE STRATEGIES

1. Avoid anyone who is sporting an unnatural tan and flip-flops; it's a sure sign they are one of the Dubai Deserters.

2. Whenever anyone starts to discuss Dubai, pass out.

3. Lecture them on how wonderful Teeside is, telling them that the new nuclear waste island project is a must buy opportunity. And if you can foam at the mouth all the better.

4. Send them a book on facing up to your debt problems.

5. Start a bounty hunting business on behalf of the Dubai authorities in which you capture Dubai Deserters and return them so they can stand trial in return for a large fee.

THE DUBAI DESERTER:

☐ Can blame someone else for their predicament

☐ Only has them self to blame

☐ Deserves our sympathy and should be hugged

☐ Deserves our contempt and should be shot

The Economic Rioter

There is a well known correlation between the severity of economic difficulty and the number of violent protests. Indeed, England has somewhat of a long tradition of mob violence when it comes to this area – The Peasants' Revolt of 1381, The Jack Cade rebellion of 1450, the 1749 gin riot, the Luddites during the Industrial Revolution, Peterloo in 1819, the poll tax riots of 1990 and not forgetting the G20 riots of 2009. As is usually the case, the protests start out peaceful enough and in many cases quite jolly with a lot of people viewing it as a nice family day out and an opportunity to prepare some rather fancy placards showing off their creative side. Then it descends into a bit of shouting and the occasional minor altercation with the authorities, plus the ubiquitous 'contained fire'. In the past this was usually followed by a brief discussion with the reigning monarch before everyone was butchered by the King's men. Roll forward a few hundred years and the King had been replaced by the government and the King's men by the police or perhaps the army but the outcome was often the same, as by this time both the police and army had guns. As one of my dear friends used to say to his intended victim before he knocked their teeth through their arse, 'my mum always told me that actions speak louder than words'. I can therefore only assume that the need to resort to physical violence is part and parcel of being British. I blame the parents as well as the education system.

During the economic turmoil of the 1980s in which Margaret Thatcher and the Tories were left to clear up the God awful mess left by the useless Labour government that preceded them, times were tough. Unemployment was into double-digits and there was even an odd reggae song about how bad the Tories were and how they should be kicked out. It was great music. In fact I recently saw The Beat on their 30th anniversary tour and they even replaced the lyrics 'Stand down Margaret' with 'Stand down Gordon' which was both topical and a nice touch. Things got progressively worse especially when the poll tax was introduced there were protests and riots in major cities all over the country. At the time I was a teenager attending a local comprehensive school (not the best in the area, but I turned out okay, thanks for asking) and during one particular lunchtime one of the many skinheads that attended this fine institution asked if I wanted to join in the riot that was going to take place that evening in the small market town in which I lived. I made my excuse that I was off to a much more significant riot in Brixton, pushed my right fist into my left palm to signify my intended use of extreme violence and left him to his own devices. Needless to say there were no riots that night, or indeed any others. In fact I had rather a good night's sleep if I remember.

As the Credit Crunch has worn on, the level of unrest has continued to grow as an increasing number of people are left with little or no option but to make their voices heard by protesting (aka rioting). This time The Economic Rioter is not just restricted to the anti-capitalist brigade who like nothing more than to smash the windows out from

a random bank or two. We are witnessing the stalwart middle classes coming out en masse to highlight a few minor concerns they have about pensions, tax rates, the bailout, the price of fish, gravy train politicians, unemployment, repossessions, the lack of allotment space, why they haven't won the lottery and so on. Of course, unlike the anticapitalists who don't wash and often get exceptionally violent, the middle class protestors tend to do things in a more congenial way. So you'll see grannies inching along with their Zimmer frames, retired gentlemen marching through the streets stark bollock naked, and middle aged mothers talking incessantly to one other and handing out cups of tea to policemen. The press love it and you can often see cameramen sporting exceptionally long lenses egging on the demonstrators to throw a brick through a window or to urinate in public so that they get an exclusive picture. In fact, if you look carefully, most of them are carrying bags full of bricks and dishing out large bottles of Coke. The same can be said of the reporters, although they are much funnier to watch, especially when you see them poo themselves as the inevitable clashes between the protestors and police get a bit out of hand. Their cheerful disposition and random banter with balaclava clad, club wielding anarchists is soon replaced with the wide-eyed look of a rabbit caught in the proverbial headlights.

Naturally, we are not alone in the recession, it is a global affair. And, just like in Britain, there are plenty of economic protests going on elsewhere that are getting out of hand; Greek farmers blocked roads and caused much commotion complaining about falling agricultural prices; French workers (who are already prone to the odd riot and setting fire to things over the most trivial of matters) protested about the lack of job protection in their country; and Icelandic demonstrators clashed with police over their now bankrupt nation. I guess they had every reason to get a bit shirty. In Germany things are likely to get a whole lot worse as they don't have a very good track record when it comes to severe economic problems … it usually leads to a right wing dictatorship and world war. After all, why fight amongst yourselves when you can invade France?

☐ **Tick here when you have spotted the Economic Rioter**

SYMPATHY RATING – **8**

One has to sympathise with the Economic Rioter. Edmund Burke, that great Tory philosopher got it right in 1796 when he said 'If the people are turbulent and riotous, nothing is to be done for them on account of their evil dispositions. If they are obedient and loyal, nothing is to be done for them, because their being quiet and contented is proof that they feel no grievance'. In other words, we lose either way. It is of course unfortunate that the inept governments of the day are so out of touch that we have no alternative but to take to the streets even if it does end up in the odd bit of violence. And although this should be never be condoned, it does make exceedingly good television and much better than the usual crap.

RARITY - 2

The frequency and severity of economic riots today is a lot less than a few hundred years ago, and they are considerably less violent. However, as it becomes patently clear to most people in the country that their futures have been flushed down the toilet we should expect to see plenty more unrest, demonstrations and of course the odd riot or two. This is especially the case during the summer months when you can riot well into the evening.

WHAT ARE THEY DOING NOW?

If not nursing their wounds from the previous riot, you will find them organising the next big economic demonstration via You Tube, MySpace and Twitter. For those who have been beaten up and detained unreasonably by the police it will be a superb opportunity to pursue their claim through the courts and make enough money to ride out the recession.

AVOIDANCE | REVENGE STRATEGIES

1. Recognise that any form of protest is an utter waste of time because those in power are far more interested in conducting smear campaigns and lining their own pockets than your particular economic plight.

2. If you do choose to engage in any kind of demonstration make sure it is peaceful, respect other people's property and be nice to the police (or else).

3. Infiltrate one of the anti-capitalist groups and act as a spy. As you find out more about their operations use your knowledge to inform the police on what to expect. If you play your cards right and no one suspects you, you may even be offered a job with MI6 who are always on the lookout for new operatives.

4. Join the Police force as now would be a good time to make pots of cash on overtime alone.

5. Organise an economic protest about the high price of junk food. Ensure than everyone who attends wears an inflatable Sumo suit. Not only will this give you lots of useful press coverage it will also cushion you against any police baton charges.

THE ECONOMIC RIOTER:

☐ Can blame someone else for their predicament

☐ Only has them self to blame

☐ Deserves our sympathy and should be hugged

☐ Deserves our contempt and should be shot

The Economically Stressed

I always used to be a bit of a worrier, but then I went into therapy and realised that it was all my parents' fault. As a result, I am a lot calmer than I used to be and I no longer wake up screaming every night or wet the bed. I count myself very fortunate, as does my wife. My time in therapy also taught me that there are a lot of people who could be considered to be natural worriers; the sensitive souls who are concerned about everything, from stranded polar bears looking bemused as they float on small ice sheets in a warm ocean to the recycling bins – did they accidently put some recyclable material in the wrong bin? They lose sleep as they worry that the Waste Gestapo from the local council are going to come knocking in the early hours of the morning.

But apart from the irrational types who worry about absolutely everything, the rank and file of the deeply worried has grown like crazy since the start of the Credit Crunch and continues to do so as the recession deepens. The Economically Stressed come from all walks of life and are behind the rising levels of anxiety, depression, stress, marital strife, affairs, substance abuse, fast driving and sales of gourmet chocolate. They are also getting no sleep as they toss and turn as their recurring nightmare of the Repo Man popping round for a cup of tea and taking away their television set causes them to soil their bed. This wave of bed soiling is behind the current surge in rubber sheet sales.

So just who are the Economically Stressed? Well, the list includes all sorts like politicians who worry about how to make ends meet on just their salary; tramps and hobos who have seen their income drop off a cliff; and champagne salesmen who longer see their product being pissed away by a bunch of loud-mouthed investment bankers. Although the list is endless, there are three worth picking out:

• *The Wall Street WAGs* who are worrying themselves to death that their gilded lives are rapidly coming to an end. The official definition of WAG is 'air-head slapper who spends too much time shopping, attending parties and having sex with anything that has both a pulse and a bulging wallet. Unable to spell their name correctly, they use a series of hand gestures and pouts to communicate'. The WAGs of the investment banking community are especially in the poo. According to a recent survey, 80% of multi-millionaires planned to cut back on gifts and allowances for extra-marital lovers. So I guess they will be getting less sex in return then. They will have to start economising like the rest of us; it's no more Pilates lessons with a private instructor, it's time to get used to doing it in crowded church halls or community centres, surrounded by the sights, sounds (and smells) of the Great Unwashed. And it's certainly time to kiss goodbye to the facials, manicures, exotic holidays, weekends away in luxury hotels and the non-stop mindless shopping. Maybe we will be seeing fewer beautiful young women flocking to London and New York in search of love and money, (well actually mainly money, because let's face it girls you only suffered the sweat, the halitosis, and the drunken sex for the money – the sex was never that great because the bankers

had a terrible problem with performance anxiety). It, of course, works both ways, as the WAGs are ditching the bankers and looking elsewhere for their kicks, mainly it has to be said in the ranks of the Nuevo Rich – the civil service. Indeed, in India it is the public servants who are getting the pick of the crop where women are concerned – the poor bankers are considered to be toxic assets.

- The *Safe but Scared*. Even though there are a few people who have been very careful with their cash and lucky enough to remain in full-time employment they too appear on the list of the Economically Stressed. Fearful that their life savings will be stolen by the government or that they will be inundated by calls from cash-strapped charities desperate to make up for the reduction in donations and their less fortunate family members, they experience regular panic attacks in which their chest tightens and they begin to hyper-ventilate as they have terrible visions of Alistair Darling dressed up as Alice in Wonderland creeping around their house looking for anything that is remotely valuable.

- The *Organised Crime Syndicate* is falling on hard times too. During the good times when there were plenty of businesses to extort, people to kidnap and kids to sell drugs to, they all managed their own patches without any interference. In fact they all seemed to get along rather well, often having barbecues together. Now that the money just isn't available anymore they have started to encroach on each other's territories in order to protect their revenues. The results speak for themselves, the odd head on the side of the road, the crackle of gunfire in the evening, and a faint smell of barbecues, although in this instance, they are barbecuing the head of a rival syndicate; still it tastes darn wonderful with a little hickory sauce.

☐ **Tick here when you have spotted the Economically Stressed**

SYMPATHY RATING – **10**

We all know that money worries trump all others, including shouting out your wife's best friend's name during intercourse, or crashing your car into the front room. Whenever money is an issue, it creates huge strains on families and is one of the primary causes of breakups. It is a shame because I always thought that people got married because they loved each other, as Tammy Wynette sang about in 'Stand by Your Man', but I was clearly wrong. Naturally I wouldn't expect people to have much sympathy for the increasingly skint crime syndicates as they will be able to look after themselves. The same is true for the poor old WAGs, or should I say, SLAGs.

RARITY – **10**

The Economically Stressed are everywhere. You can tell them apart from those who seem somewhat comfortable with the whole Credit Crunch thing, such as loan sharks, the Repo Man; retired bank bosses and the like. The ranks of the Economically Stressed will of course increase dramatically over the coming months and years as the full extent of the mess we are in is fully felt.

WHAT ARE THEY DOING NOW?
Seeking any form of medication that will help to relieve their stress, popping bottles of Prozac tablets and other sedatives so that they can at last get some sleep without waking up in a cold sweat. You can usually spot them a mile off because they seem to be in a permanent state of sedation and prone to random laughing fits.

AVOIDANCE | REVENGE STRATEGIES
1. Shun the whole money thing and find a sense of purpose in your life which is not defined by how much you have or earn. You will find it much easier to cope with the recession and you might even become less of a money obsessed bore.

2. To avoid being economically stressed, refuse to read any newspaper, watch any news or economics show which involves Gordon Brown and never open any of your credit card bills or bank statements. They always say ignorance is bliss, so why not give it a try?

3. Purchase multiple copies of the war time poster with the slogan 'Keep Calm and Carry On' and use them to decorate your house. It will really help to take your mind off your financial woes.

4. If you find yourself rocking from side to side, pulling your hair out and banging your head against the wall every time you think about your finances, then it is safe to say that you are economically stressed. Seek help immediately. However, if you are experiencing rapid heartbeats, a choking sensation, sweating, and numbness and tingling feelings in your fingers you are probably having a heart attack and will need to call 999.

5. Offer any suspected case of The Economically Stressed a nice bar of chocolate or perhaps a tin of Quality Street; it's a lovely treat and it is well known that chocolate will boost serotonin levels far better than sex ever could.

THE ECONOMICALLY STRESSED:

☐ Can blame someone else for their predicament

☐ Only has them self to blame

☐ Deserves our sympathy and should be hugged

☐ Deserves our contempt and should be shot

The Elusive Tax Evader

There is a fundamental difference between tax avoidance and tax evasion. Whilst the former involves finding legitimate ways to avoid paying the tax you owe by employing clever accountants and investment advisors, the latter is highly illegal and winds you up in jail. Ask Lester Piggott, Judy Garland, Martha Stewart or even Al Capone, who despite running a lucrative but illegal booze business during Prohibition ended up in jail simply because he evaded his taxes. If only he'd been a good citizen he would have managed to continue to run his business without any interference from the authorities and that nasty man Elliot Ness. Mind you, if he hadn't been so free and easy with his todger he may not have died of syphilis. Still I guess some people never learn.

No one likes to pay tax and they like it even less when it is wasted by brain-dead government officials who fail to use it properly. But we all know that unless we pay up, the country would be in a right old mess and we wouldn't have the National Health Service, our wonderful schooling system or a police force to beat up protestors. The country would end up being run by a bunch of crooks concerned only about their own welfare and no one else's. Normal people like you and me who work hard and pay our taxes get a little bit pissed off when we hear about those that don't pay tax (or as much as they should) because we know that it means we'll end up paying even more. Yes, ever since the dawn of time it has been the good old law abiding citizen (also known as an easy target) that ends up getting screwed. Not only do we pay for all the people who don't, can't, or won't work, but we also have to pick up the slack from those that choose to evade their taxes: The Elusive Tax Evader.

There are two types of people that don't pay their dues. The first are those that work in the black economy in which 'cash is king'. These are the unregistered taxi drivers who like to be paid in cash so that they can run two books and are known for the mugging of their fares, or the traveller who knocks on your door with a lorry load of stolen tarmac and offers to make your drive look pretty again for £200 (in cash, naturally, as they don't tend to have bank accounts or internet access). Then of course we have the drug dealers, prostitutes, kebab sellers, window cleaners and paper boys all of whom who manage to avoid paying taxes at all. As you'd expect the tax authorities are pretty clued up these days and they will often pose as customers to catch out the would-be evaders. When they have been rumbled, the authorities proceed to spend millions of pounds of taxpayers' money pursuing them in the courts to recover the £45 in unpaid tax.

The other group that seems to be rather adept at paying virtually no tax at all are the very wealthy and even corporations. Unlike our low-earning friends who will be tracked down mercilessly by the tax authorities, this group always seems to get away with their illegal behaviour without so much as a slapped wrist. Experts at using a combination of sleight of hand, a detailed understanding of tax law and their political connections,

this group can give the illusion that they are legitimately paying some tax, whilst employing a team of corrupt accountants and lawyers to shield them from the prying eyes of the tax collector and the true sum of their tax bill. Safe in the knowledge that with their money hidden in one of the many tax havens across the world, they can continue to pretend they are the model citizen rubbing shoulders with senior politicians and giving a few quid to charity every now and then. And isn't it funny that despite being at the top of the latest rich list and yet paying minimum tax, no one seems suspicious? Now perhaps it's because the tax officials are too busy pursuing taxi drivers or maybe those that run the country are happy to let their fellow public school boys (with whom they used to share more than just their lessons), get away with paying nothing.

Although for a long time the Elusive Tax Evader has been managing to get away with their criminal behaviour, times they are a-changing. Ever since the western world's economic system went into reverse and governments became more desperate to replenish their empty exchequers, being a tax dodger is no longer considered chic. In fact, such people are now considered to be engaged in economic warfare and are classified as legitimate targets for US Special Forces (who have clearly given up on finding Bin Laden). It won't be long before you hear the dulcet tones of Predators circling above the tax havens around the world waiting for the order to liquidate their target. I think once this has been televised on the small screen we'll see a remarkable uplift in tax takes in countries across the world. The only people who won't be coming clean will be the drug dealers and gangsters who are far too clever to be found out and who tend to pack far more firepower than the average greedy businessmen.

☐ **Tick here when you have spotted the Elusive Tax Evader**

*SYMPATHY RATING – **0***
It's okay to complain all you like about the goddamn taxes you have to pay, so long as you pay them. No one has the right to moan and gripe about the poor state of the economy when they spend more money on evading taxes than paying them, and with £13 trillion of untaxed wealth overseas you can see why. The Elusive Tax Evader deserves no sympathy and in fact should be strung up in public. Thank heavens that tax authorities around the world will shortly be posting naked pictures of everyone who fails to pay their taxes on the home pages of their websites.

*RARITY – **1***
Given that tax evaders do their best to hide from the public eye, it is pretty difficult to spot them at the best of times. Although one assumes that as soon as they are dobbed on by tax havens scared that they are about to become a target for US covert forces, they will quickly become law abiding citizens and own up to having made a simple accounting error. So whatever happens, it is highly unlikely

that you will spot The Elusive Tax Evader although you probably know exactly who they are.

WHAT ARE THEY DOING NOW?
Pooing their pants as they wait for the tax authorities to come knocking at their door or perhaps caravan. The mega rich who used to laugh in the face of the taxman are now actually quite scared as tax haven after tax haven caves in and tells everyone who wants to know who the evaders are. As for the taxi drivers, they are getting beaten up in one of the many secure locations along the M40 which are used to convince tax evaders that their behaviour is unreasonable.

AVOIDANCE | REVENGE STRATEGIES
1. Always pay the tax you owe. If we all did, then we would have the lowest taxes in the world, but, thanks to the Elusive Tax Evaders, we are paying the most.

2. Prepare a poster along the lines used to recruit soldiers for the Great War replete with an image of Lord Kitchener in the foreground looking very angry and pointing at you. Include a map of all the world's tax havens in the background along with the caption 'Your Country Needs You to Pay Your Tax You Tax Evading Bastard' and make sure Lord Kitchener is always pointing at you no matter what position you're in.

3. Model yourself on the 17th century Witchfinder General and hunt down all the tax evaders using whatever methods are available. Ideally you should collect them in a cage.

4. Pipe 'The Sun Ain't Gonna Shine (Anymore)' by Bob Crewe and Bob Gaudio into the prison cells of any Tax Evaders who have been caught.

5. Prepare an annual '100 Top Tax Evaders list'. Include photos, details of how much they earn, how much tax they pay, and where they hide their money alongside other interesting facts about them such as their favourite colour and which pets they had as a child.

THE ELUSIVE TAX EVADER:

☐ Can blame someone else for their predicament

☐ Only has them self to blame

☐ Deserves our sympathy and should be hugged

☐ Deserves our contempt and should be shot

The Escaping Entrepreneur

One of the interesting things about recessions is that it is a time when boldness and entrepreneurialism pays off. Being timid, cutting back on things and crying about all the bad news is not much use at all and doesn't tend to win you many friends. And although many us would like to claim that we are entrepreneurial (in the same way that nearly everyone thinks they can write a book or that they have talent), most of us are happy to work for a complete bastard who treats us like dirt rather than stick our necks out and launch a new business venture on our own. After all, if anything goes wrong you will have no one to blame but yourself which is terribly disheartening, and like the recession it's much more fun to point the finger at someone else for your predicament. Well, until you have been sacked, that is. That's when we all become reluctant entrepreneurs.

In reality, true entrepreneurial types are few and far between; they are the true generators of jobs and wealth in the country. Furthermore, most of us would be happy for them to keep hold of the money that they generate, as after all, they are not some parasitic toe rag who has backstabbed their way to the top of a corporation and milked the system for all its worth, or a politician who has claimed £100000 for an empty flat four yards from Parliament.

It would seem like a very good idea to anyone who is capable of breathing that those who can pull us out of the recession should be encouraged. Well it does to normal people, but we have to remember that the cretins who run the country don't think that way; in fact they don't think. So rather than offer every incentive possible, they have come up with a cunning scheme to soak the very people who might make things better. According to some reliable sources, when the Chancellor, the Prime Minister and a few other *clever* politicians met to discuss how to reinvigorate the crumbling economy they came up with three options:

1. Cut back on pointless government spending and waste and sack millions of civil servants.

2. Reduce state benefits for the workshy and lazy chancers who would rather watch Sky Sports all day than do a full day's work.

3. Squeeze the very life out of the country by taxing anyone who has a brain and works hard for a living.

After much thought and intensive debate the decision was made to go for option 3. The first option would never work because they would have to sack all their friends and family, and option 2 was a nonstarter because it was better to have the mass unemployed watching 'Lorraine' than rioting in the streets. So, much to the delight of left wing socialists, it was decided to target the wealth generators and soak them for as much as possible.

However, there are just one or two snags with the cunning plan. Firstly, the total mess the economy is in cannot be resolved by further soaking the small number of people who already pay the lion's share of the taxes anyway. Secondly, the hardworking entrepreneurs who prop up the economy are leaving the country by land, sea and air, in fact in any remotely useful means of transportation they can find: it's the 'Great Escape' but this time without a crack unit of the SS on their tail; just some dozy politician holding onto their ankles and begging them to stay by offering them a life peerage. And finally, anyone who earns a decent crust will simply think 'why bother?' and instead of working harder will in fact do less and begin to enjoy that wonderful thing called work-life balance they'd previously only heard about on TV and read about in the jobs section of the weekend newspapers. They can do this easily by joining the ranks of the mass unemployed where the state pays them to watch daytime television, or by joining the Civil Service where they do much the same.

☐ **Tick here when you have spotted the Escaping Entrepreneur**

SYMPATHY RATING – **9**
When it comes to earning pots of cash I think it is fair that those who genuinely earn it by a combination of hard work and building a company from scratch should be suitably rewarded. There are, of course, a whole range of people who deserve to pay, pay and pay some more. Bank bosses clearly, investment bankers too, but most of all it should be footballers who spend all day kicking a football around and when they score hugging each other and French kissing; it's wrong and should be outlawed.

RARITY – **8**
As the extent of the stitch-up is understood, the number of Escaping Entrepreneurs will increase and as taxes shoot ever upwards, it won't be long before the UK is an entrepreneur-free zone and everyone will be selling bananas in government controlled greengrocers.

WHAT ARE THEY DOING NOW?
Discussing with their accountants how to keep as much of their cash, business and any other asset which is remotely valuable outside of the country and away from the tentacles of the tax authorities. You will also see them forming orderly queues at airports and major seaports holding their one-way tickets to anywhere but here.

AVOIDANCE | REVENGE STRATEGIES
1. It's clear that showing any initiative in this country is viewed with derision and quite frankly you are better off going anywhere else, well apart

from Zimbabwe, Afghanistan, Iran, Iraq, France, Sierra Leone, Alabama or the Falkland Islands.

2. Set yourself up as an escape planning consultant, in which you devise new and interesting ways for the entrepreneur to escape the country with as much of their cash as possible.

3. Become a tax collector and roam the country looking for anyone who remotely looks as though they could be an entrepreneur. When you find them, use all manner of medieval torture techniques to wring every last penny out of them. Consider using naked flames on their feet as apparently this is highly effective.

4. Set up a rare breeds farm that caters exclusively for entrepreneurs. Ensure their enclosures include workshops, computers and white boards to recreate their natural habitat. Charge visitors a couple of pounds to get in and don't forget to include a petting area where young children can stroke the entrepreneurs in a safe tax-free environment, (always include a sink so that they can wash their hands afterwards).

5. Revisit the Roman Circus and instead of gladiators hacking lions, Christians and themselves to death, have entrepreneurs compete to retain their earnings. The idea would be very similar to the Roman games, with the entrepreneurs demonstrating their latest innovations and business ideas to a packed coliseum. The Chancellor or perhaps the Prime Minister could sit in Caesar's place and at the end of the demonstration listen to the baying mob before deciding whether the entrepreneur should be taxed at 50% or allowed to keep all his earnings. It will be far better than 'Dragons' Den' with all those arrogant and miserable tycoons telling some poor guy who has put his whole life into designing a plastic jumping turd that his idea won't fly!

THE ESCAPING ENTREPRENEUR:

☐ Can blame someone else for their predicament

☐ Only has them self to blame

☐ Deserves our sympathy and should be hugged

☐ Deserves our contempt and should be shot

The Ex, Expat

There is a lot of merit in leaving the country and starting a new life in another part of the world, the reasons to do so are possibly endless; the weather, the high cost of living; knife crime; crumbling infrastructure; lack of jobs; the poor education system and of course television. In fact, of the 207 000 people that leave the UK every year, something in the region of 87% do so because of poor quality daytime TV. Of course many of the reasons listed above are also why so many immigrants want to come to the UK, so I guess there must be something about living here that's appealing. I can imagine a revolving door at the UK border spinning at a thousand miles per hour as those fleeing the country are replaced by economic refugees and chancers from around the world, all hoping to get hold of the generous state benefits which are offered to the generally useless.

The desire to leave the country is also fuelled by the popularity of property programmes, like 'A Place in the Sun', where old folks and the newly unemployed look to leave their rundown semi in Aberdeen and live next to an opencast mine in the middle of Spain. Such programmes make the whole thing look like an absolute breeze in which the transition is portrayed as easier than going down to your local Morrisons to buy a pint of milk. Although the UK's Diaspora have started new lives in countries across the world, the majority seem to flock to Spain, France or Australia, with Spain appearing to be most popular amongst the retired. There was of course Dubai, but that's now just a sandy building site, only the clinically insane move there. I used to go to Spain on my holidays and the only thing I remember is all the fish and chip shops and pubs. I did like the crazy hats the Spanish police wore which resembled my plastic lunchbox, but I'm afraid that isn't enough of a draw for me to go back anytime soon.

Over the years little enclaves of British people have appeared as if by magic around Spanish golf courses, bowling greens and seaside towns. The British, generally not prone to mixing with the local population, have recreated their quintessentially English country villages where foreigners are banned and posters of the Queen adorn everyone's front room. And as the OAPs flocked there in their thousands, young families followed in their wake, pursuing their dream of opening a bar selling warm English ale, British food and piping in the latest football match between Man City and Portsmouth. There was no need for any of the foreign muck that the locals ate, this was the British at their empire building best. For a while this all seemed to go rather well, with everyone living quite the life of Riley: they could laugh at the constant rain on the weather forecasts and throw their empty beer cans at Tony Blair each time he came on TV.

As the recession has increased in its severity, the expat has been replaced by the Ex, Expat. It's not because the weather in the UK has suddenly improved, although global warming is certainly helping, nor is it down to the excellent way the economy is being steered through the rough fiscal seas; it's because the expat is all dried up and fresh

out of cash. Other factors of course include the worst recession in living memory, over-zealous property developers who have flooded the property market with millions of expat homes and dodgy Spanish rules which allow the authorities to take your house away on a whim and smash it up. But these are trifling worries and nothing to be overly concerned about. The dream is over for so many who thought that moving out to Spain was as good as it gets. Faced with plummeting pensions as the Pound goes the same way as the Zimbabwean Dollar and property prices fall through the floor, the poor old expats are returning in their droves. Many are quite rightly angry as their sunny lifestyles have had the stuffing knocked out of them. So to return the favour, many are walking away from their properties or reversing cement lorries into their apartments and filling them with concrete. I guess in a thousand years from now an enthusiastic archaeologist will excavate the area and try to understand everything about the people that lived there and why the expat suddenly became an ex, expat.

They are interviewed on television as they sit around their poolside, sipping sangria whilst wearing inappropriately brief swimming costumes. They talk about how many friends they have made whilst out there (none of them foreign, of course) and how they are heading back home with their dreams in tatters. The interviewer tries to remain focused and attentive as he does his best to avoid looking directly at the errant public hair sticking out from the very brief briefs.

☐ **Tick here when you have spotted the Ex, Expat**

SYMPATHY RATING – 7
It is a real shame that so many people are having to give up on their dreams and come back to the UK. Lord knows how they are going to cope when they have no money, no friends and find themselves in a small flat at the top of a grey tower block on the outskirts of Liverpool. Que sera sera.

RARITY – 5
The Ex, Expat is becoming more common and is easy to spot with their perma-tans and skin so deeply weathered from constant exposure to the midday sun you're more likely to find them in the skin cancer clinics dotted around the country, (what they thought to be beauty spots were in fact cancerous growths).

? *WHAT ARE THEY DOING NOW?*
Rationalising to anyone who will listen that the whole expat thing was just a phase they went through and that being back in the UK is so lovely and that they had forgotten what a fair, happy, well run country it was. Given that most of them probably left the last time Labour was in power and the country was going to the dogs, then it must feel like they never left.

AVOIDANCE | REVENGE STRATEGIES

1. Leaving the country is a cracking idea and one I am thinking about too – you have to when you know it's completely screwed. However, always make sure you do your homework. I would recommend completing an expat stress test before you take the plunge. Loosely modelled on the one which has been applied to the big investment banks, this will allow you to determine whether you are likely to survive the recession and will ensure that if you do leave, you will never have to come back.

2. Set up a support group for returning expats and organise events where they can show each other pictures of themselves relaxing by a pool. To make them feel at home, include a few sunlamps and offer them glasses of sangria.

3. Now that the Specials have regrouped, why not hire a van and drive round all the Brits abroad enclaves playing the classic tune, 'Ghost Town'?

4. Film a documentary entitled 'Ex, Expats Examined' in which you follow the lives of expats coming home. Play out their misery on the small screen from the point at which they finally give up on their dream (filmed in bright sunlight), through to when they arrive at a cold and wet Manchester Airport. As you film, make sure you zoom in on the tired looking wallpaper of the council house they have had to move into and cut to the tears as they run down the ex, expat's faces. You will probably win a Bafta.

5. Launch a new soap opera called 'Helldorado' which follows the lives and loves of a group of expats. Include shady characters like the dodgy estate agent and the evil government official hell bent on destroying the expat dream. Also include the ubiquitous salacious bar owner and some infirm pensioners who spend most of their time on the toilet.

THE EX, EXPAT:

☐ Can blame someone else for their predicament

☐ Only has them self to blame

☐ Deserves our sympathy and should be hugged

☐ Deserves our contempt and should be shot

The Extended (to breaking point) Family

Bringing up a family is possibly one of the hardest jobs around and much harder than most people believe. Which is why so many couples don't have kids or if they do, go back to work five days after giving birth and leave some other poor sod to bring them up. Naturally, those with plenty of cash can pack their brats off to private school where they will never actually have to see them again.

The fun of family life starts from the moment your spawn is ejected from the womb and all the pooing, crying and vomiting begins in earnest. When the sleepness nights end they are replaced by more pooing, crying and vomiting as the kids pass through the teething stage and pick up every illness under the sun from their friends at school. Then once they move into their teenage years you face yet more pooing, crying and vomiting as they get amoebic dysentery from their gap year, start and end relationships every couple of months and discover the downsides of getting bladdered on a Saturday night. And after 20 years, when they finally leave home you can at last get your life back and remember why you got married in the first place (assuming you haven't divorced by then, which is highly likely, in which case it starts all over again). Before the economy tanked you could wave goodbye to the kids as they went off to make their own way in life and you could rest easy knowing that your parents, now in their dotage, were comfortable in their sheltered housing in Bognor Regis.

Since the housing crash, the drying up of the credit markets, the inexorable rise in unemployment and the exiting of all the low paid immigrants, this wonderful family idyll has been replaced by a nightmare that would only befit an episode of 'Eastenders'. The empty nesters now face the prospect of being the Extended (to breaking point) Family in which their three bedroomed semi, which would have suited them nicely for the next 20 years is now full to capacity with any or all of the following:

• The boomerang boys and girls who, having left university with their hard earned degrees have discovered there aren't any jobs and that actually no one values degrees as much as they used to. Saddled with massive debts that now have to be paid off they have little choice other than sleeping on the streets or going back home again. Lying on the single bed in their old bedroom surrounded by their childhood toys and memories, they feel like a total failure and let down by the state. And they soon lapse into their old ways – not tidying their room, never clearing the table after dinner, playing loud music, treating their mother like a skivvy and father like a cash point and staying out until well after their bedtime playing on the swings with all their friends, who incidentally are also unemployed graduates.

- The divorcee who having been taken to the cleaners by their ex now has to come back home with their tail between their legs. As they attempt to fit their share of the possessions from the divorce into the front room (it's a shame they fought for all the white goods) it isn't long before it resembles a junk shop and the arguments start. The situation is made far worse if there are babies involved and when the dating begins.

- The 'Married But Nowhere To Go' couples whose dream of getting onto the housing ladder has been shattered by the refusal of their bank to grant them a 100% mortgage and lend them 18 times their joint income. With no choice but to save their money for a massive deposit and wait for the housing market to bottom-out they desperately try to settle into married life in a tiny room which barely fits a double bed and has murals of Mickey Mouse on the ceiling.

- The low pension parents who wrongly believed that after saving for years they would have enough money to see them through their retirement. And after having invested unwisely in a buy-to-let property found themselves mired in debt. With no choice but to sell their home to pay their debts they now depend on the largesse of their children, but consider it payback for looking after them when they were kids.

- The uncared for grandma who by virtue of all the low paid immigrants leaving the country has been booted out of her care home. Left in the corner of the room to fester, it isn't long before the faint smell of urine drifts into the kitchen and puts everyone off the rather nice chocolate sponge mum has just baked.

Of course, pooling multiple incomes and living under one roof makes economic sense, but only if you happen to be living in some massive pile with ten bedrooms. For those that don't, at least they appreciate what it must have been like living in a New York tenement building in the early part of the 20th century. Just when you thought that all the pooing, crying and vomiting was over, it starts all over again as you find yourself clearing up after your parents and grandparents.

☐ **Tick here when you have spotted the Extended (to breaking point) Family**

SYMPATHY RATING – **10**
I pity the poor sods all squashed together and living cheek by jowl. The whole joy of having a family is seeing the back of them when they are grown up, so the last thing you want is to have everyone home again. But at least they have somewhere to go and for some families, particularly mothers who often cry for weeks after their children leave home, having them back is a blessing in disguise.

RARITY – **3**
At the moment at least, the number of people who fall into the Extended (to breaking point) Family category is quite low. However, the longer the

recession drags on the more of them you will see snaking around town, kids at the front and grandma at the back, like an American chain gang.

WHAT ARE THEY DOING NOW?
Crammed around their dining room table surrounded by the paraphernalia from four generations whilst desperately trying to get on well with each other; queuing impatiently for the bathroom as Samantha insists on taking five hour baths; and spending evenings in the pub to avoid the incessant battles over who wants to watch what on television.

AVOIDANCE | REVENGE STRATEGIES
1. In these difficult times it is comforting that there is one place where your extended family will feel welcomed. When you can't rely on the government to support you and your friends are all going down the toilet, you can at least rejoice in knowing that home is where the heart is.

2. The best thing to do when your kids leave home is to move into a one bedroomed cottage. This will allow you to avoid the increasing risk of having your extended family living with you for the rest of your life. It will also give you a bit of extra cash to spend unwisely.

3. Enclose your garden with a massive sheet of tarpaulin, cover the grass with duckboard and create some makeshift rooms for the returning family members. When your neighbours kick up a fuss tell them that your family has swine flu and they are under quarantine.

4. Invite Bruce Forsyth to host a new version of the 'Generation Game' only this time restrict it to extended families living under one roof. Watch in amusement as Bruce quizzes them on the problems of grandma's incontinence.

5. Research your family tree in order to document your full set of relations and once finished invite them to live with you under one roof. With any luck you will get into the Guinness Book of Records under the 'The most people from one extended family living under one roof during a recession' category.

THE EXTENDED (TO BREAKING POINT) FAMILY:

☐ Can blame someone else for their predicament

☐ Only has them self to blame

☐ Deserves our sympathy and should be hugged

☐ Deserves our contempt and should be shot

The Financial Oracle

I do wonder if there is anyone in the world who truly understands how the financial markets work. You would imagine that after a few hundred years someone would have figured it out by now. After all we have had plenty of bubbles, depressions and recessions, peaks and troughs and there are millions of books and courses available which purport to help us mere amateurs understand what the hell is going on. Of course, the fact that no one has a clue doesn't stop those with a point of view from claiming that they, and only they, have absolute knowledge and need to be listened to.

The Financial Oracle is usually very quiet during boom times as everyone is too busy making money hand over fist and enjoying themselves to care about what they might think. You might get the odd one or two doom and gloom merchants who do nothing but complain and warn people that the world is about to end (well financially anyway). But as soon as the stock market crashes they all come out of the woodwork desperate to make a name for themselves as they predict everything from when the recession will end, to why Venezuela is going to be the next superpower, to why we are going back to the Great Depression and how it's a good idea to ditch the dollar and start using Roman coins again. They also do it because it (a) helps to sell their newly published book; (b) promotes their rather dubious investment company; and (c) allows them to make money by offering a subscription to their monthly newsletter which reveals details of the previously unheard of investment strategies of Hernandez Cortes. Such newsletters which often include an earnest photograph of the Financial Oracle on the front, are written so that a child could read them (lots of different fonts, bold lettering, plenty of red ink, the occasional graph of the stock market going up and down and a few pictures of gold bars). They also adopt a somewhat bizarre 'familiar' tone which gives you the impression that it is someone you have met down your local pub that is giving you advice you hadn't asked for; in other words advice you should never take. But no matter which one you pick up it will offer you a sure-fire way to make enough money to retire in six weeks and suggest that if you had only followed their investment strategy when they sent the same pamphlet to you six months ago you would already be halfway there. According to a number of reputable financial regulators, people who subscribe to such shite need to be lobotomised.

The Financial Oracle comes in many shapes and sizes, including:

• *The Great Depression Debater* who will promote the idea that we are all essentially screwed that the next Depression is coming and we are all going to end up living off a diet of peppercorns and freshly squeezed worms. They wear dark suits (to signify their neuroticism) and describe in a deadpan voice how the synchronised freefall of GDP, housing, consumption, and taxation will lead to a global disaster of astronomical proportions. They also like to point out smugly that they had personally written to all the global leaders two years ago to warn them that this was all about to kick off and how all those suggesting that the stock market will recover are arseholes.

- *The How to Save the World from Financial Ruin Guru* who will lay out what policies the global leaders need to pursue and why it's necessary to think outside of the box and do things that no one has ever done before. Like bailout absolutely everybody and flood the market with worthless cash. Naturally you never see these gurus discussing the issues of the day with those in power … maybe it's because they don't know what they are talking about.

- *The Investment Strategist* who having spent their entire life in finance can confidently predict the bottom of the economic cycle and when it is time to jump back into equities. Always overly optimistic, they convince people to sink cash into the markets and when it fails they switch their strategy to bonds or gold and then back to equities again. Masters of the 'bait and switch' technique to investing they sucker the investor every time and in the process do very nicely.

- *The World Has Changed Expert* who states with the surety of a prophet that capitalism is dead and things will never be the same again. When asked what will replace it, they look off into space with a blank expression and then say 'Well, I haven't got a bastard clue'.

So what can we conclude? A monkey on crack is probably just as effective at predicting how the financial markets will behave as any of the Financial Oracles. Plus it is more amusing to watch the monkey explain to you in a series of high pitched grunts that the Dow will end at 10000 by the end of the year.

☐ **Tick here when you have spotted the Financial Oracle**

SYMPATHY RATING – 4
It must be tough being a Financial Oracle as it has been statistically proven that they are 80% wrong 37% of the time and only 15% right 47% of the time. How can you rely on someone who is constantly changing their opinions?

RARITY – 10
Financial Oracles are ten to a penny. The experts who take up vast amounts of air time on the television and radio and fill newspapers with their lengthy columns, have been joined by millions of amateur know-it-alls who also believe they have the answers. Whether it is the local hairdresser who gives you an earful as you're getting your short back and sides or something for the weekend done, or your proctologist who, as he pokes around, tells you that the black hole he is currently peering into reminds him of the parlous state of the financial markets.

WHAT ARE THEY DOING NOW?
Stirring up potions containing pigs blood, dead frogs, the ground bones of Adam Smith and saliva from a couple of investment bankers and pouring it onto blotting paper to see what it tells them about the future of the financial markets.

Those less interested in witchcraft are busy writing their next insulting investment newsletter which details how the alignment of Jupiter, Pluto and Neptune signifies the most important buying signal since the Franco Prussian War of 1870–71.

 AVOIDANCE | REVENGE STRATEGIES
1. Don't listen to any Financial Oracle because they really don't know what they are talking about, apart from that Doctor Doom guy who seems spot on. I just wish he'd smile a bit more; even once would be nice.

2. Use a dice to decide what investment strategy you are going to take. I would recommend the following: if you roll a one, then put all you money into oil; if it's a two, place 30% in equities and 70% in currency swaps; if it's a three, keep all your money in a shoebox on the top of your wardrobe; if it's a four just burn it because it's worthless anyway; if it's a five put 95% into government bonds and the rest in a local taxi business and if it's a six put it all into an interesting sounding hedge fund.

3. Drive around the financial districts of major cities playing Bachman-Turner Overdrive's classic hit – 'You Ain't Seen Nothing Yet'.

4. Create your own investment strategy and call it the 'Quantum Approach to Wealth Generation'. Base it on the combination of Heisenberg's Uncertainty Principle (where you can either know where the money is or its value, but not both) and Schrödinger's Cat (where money replaces the cat) and launch a subscription only monthly newsletter that reveals how it works.

5. Write to all the world's Financial Oracles and ask them to explain why their investment knowledge and strategies are better than everyone else's. Publish the answers in a book called 'Financial Oracles at War' and see if you can sell the film rights to Steven Spielberg.

THE FINANCIAL ORACLE:

☐ Can blame someone else for their predicament

☐ Only has them self to blame

☐ Deserves our sympathy and should be hugged

☐ Deserves our contempt and should be shot

The Frightened Fat Cat

Although I am sure there are plenty of frightened fat cats of the furry variety out there, (which given the tide of feline obesity is unsurprising), I am of course referring to the human 'Fat Cat', often called chief executive officer, or CEO. The Fat Cat is, well, fat. The latest research found that 61% of male bosses were overweight against a national average of 41% so the question we need to ask ourselves is – do Fat Cats get overweight before or after they become a big boss? I think this would make a great exam question as part of an MBA programme.

But apart from the width of their typically unhealthy girth, they are fat in every sense of the word. Fat Cats have a bloated sense of their own self-importance, their bank accounts overflow with more cash than the GDP of Papua New Guinea and they must own every trapping that clearly demonstrates they are wealthier than anyone else – even other Fat Cats. The Fat Cat is usually the product of a poor childhood; brought up on the back streets of a long since defunct northern industrial town. This kind of background spurs them on to prove to all their family members and the odd stranger or two (that used to beat the living daylights of them as a child), that they have 'done good'. Once in their position of power they live in oversized properties furnished with crass items such as gold shower curtains, Italian marble flooring and handmade green wallpaper. They use their vast amounts of cash to feed their addiction to wealth, drugs and sports cars; buy up football teams and improve the lot of their offspring by passing them the company's cash so they don't feel left out. And just to make sure they can keep the lucre flowing they employ their toadying mates as non-executive directors who in turn unquestioningly agree to outlandish requests for yet more money, share options and lavish pension plans.

The Fat Cat loves the public eye and seeks it out, either by attendance at self congratulatory charity events, by engaging in public spats with the chief executives of companies they are taking over, by purchasing honours from their local Member of Parliament, or by starting messy tabloid headline-inducing divorces with their bitter ex-wives. The Fat Cat is indeed larger than life. But then they need to be in order to stop their massive sense of self-loathing from eating them alive.

For years the tabloid press has harped on about Fat Cats and how their incomes and lifestyles are quite frankly unjustifiable when so many of their staff are paid less than a living wage. The riposte from the Fat Cats and those that represented them is that 'it is important to pay for talent'. And without massive paycheques, call girls and Aston Martins, top executives and CEOs would leave the country to go and work for a crazy dictator on the other side of the world. As you'd suspect, the Fat Cats lapped it up in the same way our feline friends lap up a bowl of cream.

You can usually spot the Fat Cat by the words and phrases they use, things like: 'Do you know who I am?'; 'And what job do you do, little man?'; 'The $450 million pay

package is justified, despite the company going into liquidation'; and 'I wouldn't get out of bed for anything less than $1 million'. For a long time, the Fat Cats have pranced around with their egos at least 50 yards ahead of their physical body (which is going some), believing themselves to be untouchable. But in the same way that syphilis and Elliot Ness caught up with Al Capone, the poor Fat Cat has been rumbled.

The credit crunch has turned the Fat Cat into a Frightened Fat Cat too scared to walk down any dimly lit street at night or open the post. They now cower behind their curtains watching out for the next lynch mob to march down their tree-lined avenue, hell bent on smashing up their Porsches and throwing a few well aimed bricks through the windows of their mansion. As their companies go to the wall, the 'you have to pay for talent' mantra is being replaced by 'It's not my fault' as it turns out the Fat Cat clearly had no idea how to run their company in the first place. Indeed, during the good times, they would be more than happy to claim the success of their business was down to them, but during the lean times – well that's when they develop a deep sense of amnesia and lose their backbone. They go very quiet and refuse to accept responsibility. Fat Cats are finding that they are no longer walking on water, but drowning in guano. Their human frailties are brought into sharp relief by protestors who hold placards with words like 'criminal' written on them. Or they are publicly-humiliated, questioned by Rottweiler reporters or incompetent politicians (who are often former Fat Cats themselves, adding to the irony). No longer the kings of commerce they once were, the Fat Cats shuffle away like so many of the minions they once drubbed and bullied at work.

☐ **Tick here when you have spotted the Frightened Fat Cat**

SYMPATHY RATING – **2**
Although it is perhaps a tad unfair to blame every single CEO for the economic crises, as there are probably at least four who are nice, there are plenty out there who have been happily feeding at the trough for years, demanding bigger and bigger salaries for poorer and poorer results. Even when they make a generous gesture like not taking a salary at all, they still award themselves huge bonuses (based upon the inverse square of their company's performance) equivalent to two or three medium sized houses or 12 family cars. The fact that they are now being targeted is of course a shame, but not that much.

RARITY – **3**
The Frightened Fat Cat is actually quite rare and is mainly restricted to the banking community, where salaries, arrogance, aloofness and incompetence were once high. However, as more and more pissed off employees, pensioners, investors and politicians get onto the Frightened Fat Cat bandwagon we should expect to see lots more of them. That said of course, we may already have seen the peak as politicians generate new laws to tax Fat Cats to death. This could be the only sensible way to pay off the huge public debt we are now saddled with.

WHAT ARE THEY DOING NOW?

Taking extended holidays on their yachts, or private and heavily guarded tropical islands, well away from the tabloid press and angry mobs of protestors. From the safety of some far flung destination they can claim innocence, appear surprised and start penning their memoirs ...'How I made skip loads of cash whilst screwing the business, by F. Cat Esquire'.

AVOIDANCE | REVENGE STRATEGIES

1. Find a job in a company where the CEO earns less than three times your salary. You may have to emigrate to a Nordic country where everyone is nice to each other to achieve it, but I am sure you will enjoy the change in lifestyle and you will fell far less angry than you do today.

2. Write to your MP to demand the imposition of Super Tax on anyone who earns more than you.

3. Open a home for Frightened Fat Cats offering a secure environment, en-suite mock-Rococo bathrooms and saucers of double cream.

4. Join one of the many groups who are busy trashing the property of the Fat Cats, although do be careful because vandalism is a criminal offence.

5. Write a children's book entitled 'The Little Frightened Fat Cat' which tells the tale of Felix the Fat Cat and warns the little darlings of the dangers of excessive egos and overeating. Include characters like Peter, the Pompous Politician, Robert the Rottweiler Reporter and Simon the Shat-Upon Supervisor, and retain merchandising rights.

THE FRIGHTENED FAT CAT:

☐ Can blame someone else for their predicament

☐ Only has them self to blame

☐ Deserves our sympathy and should be hugged

☐ Deserves our contempt and should be shot

The Good Lifer

As a child I used to love watching the television sitcom, 'The Good Life'. Set in the 1970s, it was based on Tom and Barbara Good giving up a conventional middle class existence and replacing it with a sustainable, simple and self-sufficient lifestyle whilst remaining in their suburban home. They converted their front and back gardens into allotments, grew fruit and vegetables, let loose chickens, pigs, and other assorted animals, generated their own electricity using animal waste and made their own clothes. Their neighbours, Margot and Gerry, were as you would expect, a couple of middle class snobs who proved to be the ideal sparring partner to the Goods as they struggled to eke out a frugal existence, spurning the typical middleclass trappings. It was funny, mainly because it represented an existence few were prepared to try – apart from a minority of people who owned allotments, (principally old men that smelt of mints and wee). A far cry from 'self-sufficiency' most peoples' concept of 'the good life' involved multiple foreign holidays, McMansions, a fleet of sports cars and a cellar stocked full of fine wines.

How things change. As the Credit Crunch has worsened we have witnessed an explosive growth of people embracing the tenets of 'the good life': it's back to basics on absolutely everything. Now that families have less cash to spend they are rushing headlong into a newfound existence where it's out with the old and in with the worn out.

Typical Good Lifer behaviour includes:

• Digging up any unused or derelict ground and converting it into an allotment. It's all the rage and there are already campaigns to literally dig the country out of recession run by either the National Trust, those who lived through the last war, or, predictably, desperate celebrity chefs who need extra income now that everyone has given up paying extortionate prices for a bit of fancy food served up on a hollowed out tree trunk. Even the US President's wife, Michelle Obama, has dug up the grounds of the White House to plant fruit and veg (although I would worry about the odd terrorist planting more than just an Aubergine if I were her). People across the nation are buying seeds like never before (much to the delight of the seed providers who are milking this for all its worth, introducing seed collections with catchy names like 'Garden for Victory Seed Collection ... Win the war in your own backyard against high supermarket prices and non-local produce'), and busy planting peas, runner beans and potatoes to save some cash which by all accounts amounts to well in excess of £45.67 over 12 months. Seeking out any book knocked out by supposed 'experts' on self-sustainability: making cold, rancid meat taste good with a bit of dripping and plenty of Habanero sauce, or the latest domestic goddess who is able to turn some manky bread, rotting fish and hardened cheese into a three course gourmet meal for six.

• Rushing out to department stores to purchase sewing machines and various trimmings, fabrics and knitting wools so that they can practice their mend-and-make-do

skills on their kids' clothing, much to the poor children's horror. Apparently there is now a generation of school kids wearing poorly darned clothing in mismatched colours and shoes with cereal boxes as soles. It has gotten so bad that many schools are now considering making the 'Good Life' style their official uniform.

- Getting all watery eyed as they reacquaint themselves with the foods of their childhood, such as Birds Eye Custard (26% increase in sales), Bisto Gravy (20% increase), pick 'n' mix sweets (the last bag from the now defunct Woolworths chain sold for £14 500 at auction) and Hovis loaves. It won't be long before they will be sending out their kids to run down cobbled streets in clogs to get produce from an old fashioned store where everything is left in the open to rot. Even Marks and Spencer is getting in on the nostalgia kick by offering jam sandwiches for 75p (mind you, for two bits of bread and some jam, 75p looks extortionate; so much for the credit crunch!).

- Turning to the War Generation to ask their advice on which darning techniques are best applied to a deeply soiled pair of underpants, and which type of curtain material makes the best business suit. Naturally the older generation likes to be thought of being useful and are enjoying the new found attention. Apparently massive queues are developing outside old people's homes across the nation as the need to rekindle the lost art of crocheting is becoming an urgent and important need.

Of course, none of the above has anything to with the 'good life' whatsoever as if it did we would have done it years ago. The only reason for all this nonsense is the recession. And let's face it, those that are embracing it now will be the first to ditch it when the housing market recovers and they can squeeze that extra bit of spending out of their credit cards. After all, who on earth wants to spend hours in the baking sun or driving rain planting a packet of tiny seeds in order to yield a few scrawny maggot-infested potatoes? Ultimately, the only reason it is being so enthusiastically embraced is to give the middle classes a new 'hot topic' to discuss at their Mend-and-Do dinner parties now that house prices are a non sequitur. It's all a bit dull really.

☐ **Tick here when you have spotted the Good Lifer**

SYMPATHY RATING - 4
When faced with a dwindling income something has got to give. So it's out with eating out and in with eating leftovers, mending worn out clothes and living off a diet of beetroot and potatoes. Sure one can be sympathetic, but have you ever been around people who eat nothing but vegetables ... fruity to say the least!

RARITY - 3
Despite what the press likes to tell us, this 'good life' trend is still quite limited. In the end no one can really be bothered with all the work associated with mending and doing and breaking up massive clods of clay in order to grow a few sprouts. Plus, if those embracing it sat down and worked out the actual costs

associated with all the extra effort they would realise it is far cheaper to pop down to Primark or Wal-Mart and get a new wardrobe for less than a Fiver. Not only is it cheaper, but it will also help to stimulate the economy and it also avoids unnecessary trips to Accident and Emergency when your thumb is lacerated by your new sewing machine.

WHAT ARE THEY DOING NOW?

Foaming at the mouth as they extol the virtues of the simple life to their friends and neighbours and ruining their otherwise peaceful neighbourhood with the infernal row of chickens, pigs, agricultural machinery and the non-stop whirring from the home made wind farm.

AVOIDANCE | REVENGE STRATEGIES

1. Let it wash over you as it is yet another trendy middle class preoccupation that will eventually peter out, a bit like shell suits in the 1980s.

2. Support the idea, after all a bit of physical labour does wonders for your serotonin levels which will be welcome when your back pain becomes unbearable.

3. Don't bother giving your old clothes and unwanted goods to the charity shops, hold a jumble sale and sell the stuff direct to the general public. Use the proceeds to treat yourself to some new clothes from a high-end fashion chain store.

4. Walk around allotments wearing the Dead Kennedy's tee-shirt 'Give me Convenience or give me Death' offering supermarket vouchers for discounted fresh produce recently arrived from Kenya and Costa Rica.

5. Set a new trend – call it the Medieval Life. Make it realistic by holding demonstrations on how to cook lichen and craft hair shirts. Better still, why not ask the National Trust to sponsor you?

THE GOOD LIFER:

☐ Can blame someone else for their predicament

☐ Only has them self to blame

☐ Deserves our sympathy and should be hugged

☐ Deserves our contempt and should be shot

The Gravy Train Politician

One thing that continues to fascinate me is why anyone wants to go into politics. Perhaps it's an ego thing or maybe it's because they like talking utter shite and never answering a direct question. It might even be because that they actually want to do some good. But no, I think I know and I guess you do to. It's for all those perks and cushy numbers, for all those opportunities to line their pockets; develop their property empires at the taxpayer's expense; secure lucrative book deals; join the speaking circuit and ultimately to gain a peerage and a place in the dinosaurs' graveyard, (known colloquially as the House of Lords).

Politicians do not live in the real world even if they like to claim they do. They live in a rarified environment where, apart from lots of name calling, pointless bickering and a bit of backstabbing, they have little to do. Apart, that is from figuring out how best to max out on their allowable expenses; the kind which would land you or I in jail if we ever attempted to claim the same sort of thing at work. In fact in these financially-strapped times, claiming the cost of a Mars Bar without a receipt is likely to be a sackable offence. The fact that anyone in public service is allowed to purchase soft furnishings and fancy white goods with mine, or indeed anyone else's hard earned cash, beggars belief; Bernie Ebbers would be proud. The Gravy Train Politician knows more tricks than a bone fide member of the Magic Circle, including:

- Employing their wives, sisters, pet rabbits, elderly and infirm grandparents, or halfwit sons and daughters to help them with the important work they are doing
- Claiming a second home allowance when their house is within walking distance of Parliament
- Using their second home allowance to play and win on the property market and banking all the profits
- Claiming for everything from hanging baskets, new TVs, bathrobes, mattresses, and church donations to mock Tudor beams, granite worktops, horse manure, piano tuning, pizza wheels, the occasional porn film (they need some relief from all that hard work I guess) and the odd plug (which they patently cannot afford on their ministerial salaries)
- Offering narcissistic businessmen the opportunity to gain a peerage in return for a skip full of cash
- Ensuring their pension plans are gold bottomed instead of no-bottomed like the rest of us.

For those who come clean (i.e. who are exposed by the Daily Telegraph) there is usually a period of hand wringing followed by claims of innocence or ignorance. They were only claiming what they were allowed and were operating within the spirit of parliamentary rules. None of the perpetrators would ever knowingly do anything wrong,

surely there must have been some mistake? If I recall, the 'I was only obeying orders' plea from Nazi war criminals wasn't considered an effective defence at the Nuremberg trials and did little to prevent them enjoying a long drop with a short stop.

For those lucky few who are able to graduate into the European Parliament, the opportunity to fill their boots continues at a whole new level. Not only do their allowances eclipse their salary by three times, they can claim two fully furnished rent-free offices, more money for having an office in their constituency, a generous daily allowance for food, taxis, call girls (or boys) and so on. And remember, no receipts are required, so it's spend, spend spend! This isn't so much the gravy train, but the express gravy train, and just like Eurostar, it runs a lot faster in Europe than in the UK.

And finally we shouldn't forget that there are plenty of opportunities to make it big after the Gravy Train Politicians have finished their important work running 'matters of state'. No chance of receding into obscurity. So it's time to sell their memoirs, (no matter how crushingly dull, rambling and meaningless they might be); sit on the boards of directors of major arms dealers, investment banks or other high-paying organisations (thereby helping their buddies get lucrative contracts and pick-up obscene amounts of cash); take on important international roles, like 'Special Envoy for the Moral Backbone'; go on the lecture circuit and relive all the mind-numbing decisions they ever took. If they are very lucky, they can get their wife to publish their memoires too; two books for the remainder pile are always better than one. In any case, so long as it keeps bringing in the cash, they don't care what they do. I actually think prostitutes have more pride than politicians. Enough already!

☐ **Tick here when you have spotted the Gravy Train Politician**

SYMPATHY RATING – **0**
In these troubled times, the last thing any of us want to see is yet another spineless politician who lacks the moral courage to do the right thing telling us how much they understand our plight whilst their pockets bulge with misappropriated cash and unjustifiable allowances. The Gravy Train Politician has demonstrated they have no scruples whatsoever: anyone with a child's understanding of right and wrong would know not to act as they have. They probably look in the mirror and say to themselves '...because I'm worth it.'

RARITY – **9**
The Gravy Train Politician is very common. Their empathetic smiles as they shake hands with feral youths from sink estates are as false as their expense claims

WHAT ARE THEY DOING NOW?
If they are not attempting to justify their latest ruse for doubling or tripling their income, you will find them in focus groups dreaming up the latest

way to squeeze even more money out of the system. For those who can't take the pressure anymore (poor little darlings) they are giving up their seats in Parliament and complaining that their constituents are being nasty and unkind to them. And as they leave office, they still make pathetic attempts at justifying their thieving behaviour.

AVOIDANCE | REVENGE STRATEGIES
1. Just sit back and let it wash over you, the country is going to the dogs, and soon there won't be any money left for the Gravy Train Politician to misappropriate

2. Establish a gambling syndicate in which punters place their bets on which politician will claim the most expenses at the end of the year. See if William Hill will provide you with some free advice on how best to work out the odds. If you are feeling particularly ambitious why not publish a form book to help you follow your 'favourite' MP and work out who to place bets on

3. Withhold a portion of your annual tax bill and when challenged tell the taxman that it represents the hypothecated share of your tax burden used to lavish all the freebees on the politicians. With any luck they won't know what you are talking about and you will get away with it

4. Abolish parliament, and bring back an autocratic monarchy hell-bent on eliminating corruption

5. Launch a new board game called Gravy Train Politician – at the Pig Trough. The objective is to spend as much money as possible, with the winner being the one who has claimed the most. The game will involve following your favourite MPs as they navigate through the parliamentary allowance system. Include Share the Allowances cards which itemise the things they can claim as well as Tabloid Exposé cards which results in them having to repay some of the money back. Do not pass Go, but help yourself to £200.

THE GRAVY TRAIN POLITICIAN:

☐ Can blame someone else for their predicament

☐ Only has them self to blame

☐ Deserves our sympathy and should be hugged

☐ Deserves our contempt and should be shot

The Grumpy Undergraduate

A long, long time ago in a galaxy distant to ours, those people who were clever enough and were willing to work a little bit harder than your average Joe, were lucky enough to go to university for free. Not only did they have their tuition fees paid for them by their benevolent government, but they also had some beer money (in the form of a 'grant') thrown in for good measure. They could while away the hours staring blankly at the blackboard as a tank-top wearing lecturer droned on about some very important subject, all the while dreaming of getting into the knickers of the nubile young student sitting two rows in front. And if they put in a modicum of effort, they could get a half decent degree at the end of it.

Up until recently, time spent at university could be considered your salad days, the last throw of the youthful dice before the grinding, soul destroying monotony of work set in for the next 40 years. As an undergraduate, you didn't have to worry too much about anything, Sure you had to work and Finals were always a stressful experience, but apart from that you were free and safe in the knowledge that on graduation you could secure a good job and look forward to a lucrative career – maybe in banking if you were willing to sell your soul and be an arsehole. So long as you didn't blow your grant on a new stereo as soon as you arrived or urinate it away down some dingy side alley during term time, you could get by and leave university debt free. Being an undergraduate was great and although you had to put up with substandard housing, and the occasional menial summer job, you were a happy bunny because you always knew this was going to be a temporary existence. And if you were politically motivated and spent most of your time playing at being a socialist or right wing extremist, protesting in front of the Union Building holding placards heck, you could even come out with a degree.

Undergraduates today are anything but happy. In fact they are a miserable bunch, always complaining about something or other. The root cause of their issues is of course the tin-pot notion that everyone should have a degree which means that as well as being meaningless, a degree can no longer be paid for by the government, and ultimately the taxpayer. Of course, in the olden days when only a few people went to university (mainly it has to be said because they were lazy, good for nothing upper middle class layabouts and were broadly unemployable), the taxpayer was blissfully unaware that their hard earned cash was being pissed away every Friday night at the Level 5 Disco. Today however, with so many students pursuing their university careers, the money has run out and so they have to pay because the taxpayer won't – they are too busy paying for the pensioners, the failed health service, poor schooling and so on (thank you Mr Blair and Brown, we really appreciate your excellent stewardship of the economy). So our poor undergraduates now not only have to fork out for their tuition fees, but also need to pay for their accommodation and God forbid, their beer too. So instead of getting bladdered every night, most are working their socks off in fast food joints desperately trying to make ends meet; or if they are drinking, making half a pint

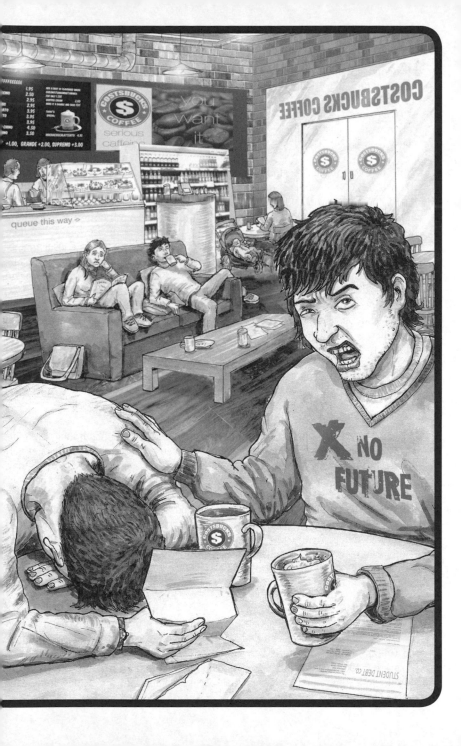

of lemonade shandy last seven hours. As University Chancellors insist on raising tuition fees even further, no doubt to pay their overinflated six figure salaries, it just gets worse for the poor undergraduate. The university lecturers don't fare too well either, as the extra money never seems to go into their pockets. Still, at least they have a job that entails working just 30 weeks a year and allows them to eye up all the young talent; they would have to pay a lot of money for that elsewhere.

By the time they finish their studies, the Grumpy Undergraduates are saddled with debts of up to £37000 (or more if they can't control their spending) which kind of screws their futures somewhat. Not only do they have to pay all this back (unless of course they go bankrupt, which is a popular pastime these days), but it also stops them from buying a house, starting a family and saving for their old age. It also forces them into those career choices that will give them loads of cash such as banking, consultancy, or if they are especially dull, boring and without ambition, accountancy. On top of this, they realise that everyone has a degree these days which makes their hoped-for gilded career look more like a straightjacket. The supposed lifetime earnings fillip of £400000 has dropped to a paltry £50000 – well worth it. So what do many of them do? They go and study some more, picking up a Masters Degree or a PhD which costs them even more money and still makes little or no difference to their future. At least they can have all their certificates framed and hang them up in the toilet.

☐ **Tick here when you have spotted the Grumpy Undergraduate**

SYMPATHY RATING – **4**

Although the poor old undergraduate likes to bitch about their lot in life, the world is actually a better place because of it. In the past, ideologically and violently minded students would protest about the issues of the day: The Vietnam War, The oppressive Chinese regime, Barclays Bank supporting Apartheid, nuclear bombs, the Poll Tax, or how the Miners were getting the crap kicked out of them by the riot police simply because they could and they had time on their hands Today, all they protest is about themselves, about how poor they are and how ripped off they have been by the government. Unlike the protests of the past, when perhaps one or two of the general public agreed with them, today no one gives a toss, they have far more important things to think about – like being able to earn a living or eat.

RARITY – **10**

Apart from the lucky boys and girls whose university education is paid for by mummy and daddy and who can as a result have a corking time, the Grumpy Undergraduate is very common. The happy-go-lucky smiles have been replaced by the tired hangdog expression you tend to find on people who have been working in a mind numbing job for decades; so I guess they are getting some early practice in.

WHAT ARE THEY DOING NOW?
If they are not marching on yet another protest complaining about tuition fees and the plight of poor students, they will be sitting in Starbucks sipping their caramel macchiato lamenting the day they chose to go to university.

AVOIDANCE | REVENGE STRATEGIES
1. Always keep away from university students, they will only make you even more depressed than you already are and leave a lot to be desired in the personal hygiene department.

2. Suggest to anyone considering going to university to forget it unless (a) their parents will pay; (b) they can secure sponsorship from a very generous employer; or (c) they can self-fund it by selling crack cocaine.

3. Seek to make university education out of the reach for anyone but the elite who can afford it – after all that's how it used to be.

4. Draw up a list of what else you could do with £37 000 and post it on university notice boards.

5. Remind them that when they graduate they will be earning little more than a paper-boy with a small number of low grade GCSEs.

THE GRUMPY UNDERGRADUATE:

☐ Can blame someone else for their predicament

☐ Only has them self to blame

☐ Deserves our sympathy and should be hugged

☐ Deserves our contempt and should be shot

The Humbled (but still incredibly wealthy) Bank Boss

When I was a young man at university, my compatriots and I used to discuss what we might end up doing after we graduated. Some of them said they wanted to be bankers, and as I was hard of hearing I am sure they said wankers. Well, I guess I must have been right. As the Credit Crunch wore on, the question of who was to blame became one of the utmost importance. Everyone wanted to blame someone; whether it was the politicians who allowed this to happen; the immigrant worker doing the jobs that no one else in the country would ever do even if their life depended on it, the reckless consumer maxed out on their credit cards; or the bankers themselves who were so overwhelmed with greed that they would sell any old dross to anyone, so long as it got them their bonus. Of course, everyone has played their part, but the villain of the piece is of course the overpaid banker. The people who are worth singling out for special treatment, however, are the bank bosses who presided over the meltdown and always claim to have been taken by complete surprise at what happened – that is until the risk manager they sacked for raising the potential problem with them in the first place goes to the press.

In my day (well, when I was younger anyway), the bank boss was a boring, one-dimensional crusty old man with halitosis and limited personality; and if I recall correctly, often alcoholic. They were the products of decades spent in their respective banks, learning their trade and carefully managing their risks (in other words not lending to anyone who looked remotely untrustworthy, which was nearly everyone). Today however, they are larger than life, extraordinarily well paid, arguably have a lot more personality but clearly little knowledge of how banking actually works. I think most of them majored in media studies, as this is about the only thing they seem to be good at these days, given how much time they seem to spend in front of the press.

Their lot has not been a happy one of late. Having brought their institutions to their knees they have gone into hiding with massive payoffs, huge pensions and little concern for the damage they have done to their businesses or of course the wider economy. Even as banks collapse before our eyes, the bank boss still feels it is necessary to have one last roll of the dice by paying out billions in bonuses and ensuring their personal fortunes are safe and sound, like signing it all over to their wives and mistresses. And as the same banks are bailed out, their former bosses have retreated to their piles in

the countryside to play cricket and figure out how they will spend their retirement; keeping out of the public eye would seem like a good start.

Not being allowed to get away scot free of course, the bank bosses have been brought before Select Committees to be given a roasting or two by MPs who, like most politicians, have time on their hands. Talk about bolting the door well and truly after the horses have left not only the stable, but also the farm. As they walk to the meeting they resemble the cast from 'Reservoir Dogs', although in this instance with names like Mr Incompetence, Mr Brain-dead, Mr Inept, Mr Stupid and Mr Ring Piece. And as they sat before the MPs, like school boys who have just been found smoking behind the bike sheds, they were unable to offer any decent reasons as to why they screwed up so royally, and ended up blaming the Americans, the weather or indeed anything but their own ineptitude. Even those bosses who were warned about the impending doom chose to ignore the guys whose job it was to stop them doing stupid things, and in most cases just sacked them; I guess stupid is what stupid does. In the end, all they can do is turn to each other and say 'That's another fine mess you've got me into'. Still, that seemed to satisfy the politicians. Naturally, after their public drubbing, the humbled bank boss walks away with a warm feeling inside, because they still have millions in the bank and bloated pension pots which they refuse to give back. And who cares about losing the knighthood, it only cost a couple of grand to buy anyway.

The same thing of course is happening in America, although after years of spending money on antique rubbish bins, and paying themselves the equivalent of Guinea Bissau's Gross Domestic Product, they are being rounded up like dogs, tried and sent to jail in orange jumpsuits with industrial-sized chains around their ankles – rich man walking. And, I guess if this kind of thing happened in China, you would never see them again. Thank heavens for the British Justice system; arseholes.

☐ **Tick here when you have spotted the Humbled (but still incredibly wealthy) Bank Boss**

SYMPATHY RATING – 1
Apparently, being a bank boss these days is on par with being an international terrorist and those who have long since lorded it over the rest of society are now too embarrassed and ashamed to be associated with banking. Still, as embarrassed as they may be, I am sure they won't be losing too much sleep as they cruise around the Mediterranean on their luxury yacht, while their employees are kicked out of their jobs, and their customers lose their livelihoods and houses. Nice work if you can get it.

RARITY – 2
With most of the banks in state hands these days, and the bank boss baiting season nearly over, I am sure we won't see too many of this rare species

around. If you are lucky you might spot the odd Humbled Bank Boss on the cricket pitch being bowled out for a duck or in your local branch of Marks and Spencer's doing their weekly food shopping and chatting up the old hag at till number three.

WHAT ARE THEY DOING NOW?
Walking around their mansions like lost puppies, not knowing what business to screw up next. Or hanging around their wife like a bad smell getting under her feet and generally being a pain in the arse; I guess some things never change.

AVOIDANCE | REVENGE STRATEGIES
1. Only ever bank with people who you can trust and where the bank boss is a boring one-dimensional, crusty old man with halitosis and zero personality. He may even offer you a swig from his whisky bottle stashed in the top drawer of their desk.

2. Revert back to a pastoral existence based upon bartering and a simple exchange of goods and services, this way you will never be impacted by the largesse of the bank boss ever again.

3. Tar and feather the bank bosses and march them from town to town to atone for their stupidity.

4. In order to assess their innocence, use Trial by Water in which the bank boss is weighted with stones and cast into a deep river. If they float and survive, they must be guilty and jailed for life, but if they sink and drown, they are innocent and their soul will be cleansed.

5. Nationalise all banks and let the politicians run them; hmm, that sounds like a recipe for disaster ... too late, it's already happened!

THE HUMBLED (BUT STILL INCREDIBLY WEALTHY) BANK BOSS:

☐ Can blame someone else for their predicament

☐ Only has them self to blame

☐ Deserves our sympathy and should be hugged

☐ Deserves our contempt and should be shot

The Irate Investor

The whole idea of any investment is to accrue some decent returns and make your money work hard for you. If you are a lazy sort who can't be bothered, you will either spend everything you've got or just pop it into the building society and let it grow by an infinitesimal amount per year, (and then wonder why it is near enough worthless when you take it out again). But for those who don't fancy the 'Steady Eddy' approach to investing there is always the more risky and potentially lucrative path which involves placing your money elsewhere. And to help us invest our money wisely there is a whole army of financial advisors and investment managers ready and willing to help (how kind). Like investment bankers they are expert at generating new ways to make huge returns on the investments we make. And when compared to the prospect of getting virtually nothing from the poxy building society, the alternatives always seem to be very exciting which of course makes them such an easy sell. Like most things associated with finance and investing, everyone assumes that investments will always rise and never fall and despite all the small print which informs us that past performance is no guarantee of future returns we rush headlong into the deal without giving it a second's thought. And while everything is fine and dandy we just sit back and watch the fabled money tree work its magic. It's funny; as soon as you have signed up for the investment you never hear anything from your friendly advisor ever again, apart from when they have another investment you need to consider.

However, we really should have read and understood that small print because every now and then we get a reminder that many of the investments we have made are nothing short of rubbish and instead of making loads of money they end up losing us loads instead. Surely having seen the wreckage of past cock-ups they should've known better. Like pensions mis-selling where people in decent pension schemes were convinced to chuck them in and invest their money in the financial markets instead (only to lose everything), or the big endowment con where insurance giants sold homeowners one of the biggest lemons in history which paid out hefty commissions to the sales people but saddled the poor homeowners with not much apart from a mortgage that wasn't going to be paid off anytime soon. More recently we have had the split capital investment trusts and structured products which have proved to be equally useless. The only people that did benefit were, of course, those that died. So what can we learn from this? Very simply that most investors are idiots and the people that sell financial products are conmen selling a dream and delivering a nightmare.

As we enter another recession we find ourselves yet again holding investments which are a load of old bollocks and if not completely worthless then certainly worth a lot less than we invested in them. And as you'd expect, we bitch, complain and write irate letters to the money sections of newspapers about how we have been conned and ask why the investment community can be allowed to sell us such crap or ever be trusted again. Sure, we might have been told that the investment was risky but it's just not fair

that we have lost some or all of our money. Investors everywhere are seething and taking matters into their own hands. Class actions are being launched against financial institutions and financial advisors are being targeted by groups of irate investors who roam the streets, pitchforks in hand hunting down the advisor who mis-sold them their sure-fire, risk-free investment. And once more the credibility of the financial sector is in the shit-can.

Of course, it's not just the individual investor that's livid right now, there are thousands of shareholders who are feeling equally peeved. Like the pensioner who was sold a dodgy investment that was designed to see them through their retirement, the shareholder believes they were sold a dog when they were told the CEO of 'ABC Plc' knew exactly what they were doing and that investing in the company was a no-brainer; even a moron could see that. Well, the moron it seems was the shareholder who sunk thousands into the stock only to see it drop by 90% – so not so much of a no-brainer as a no-brained investment. Not one to take this lying down, the shareholders are ganging up and going mob handed to the annual general meetings to make themselves heard. If the shouting and screaming doesn't work, they resort to throwing shoes, coins, cameras, chairs and a range of ninja fighting weapons at the CEO and the rest of the board who are led off stage by 50 security guards. Although such events are good for the soul and at least make you feel better, we all know that any protests are pointless because no one cares about the shareholders.

Of course, when the markets finally recover you can guess what happens next. We all develop a case of selective amnesia. We visit new, improved and heavily regulated financial advisors, and listen to their silver tongued presentations of the latest way to make our money 'work for' us. We just can't wait to sign-up for the investment of a lifetime.

☐ **Tick here when you have spotted the Irate Investor**

*SYMPATHY RATING – **7***
I have every sympathy for the Irate Investor as they feel quite rightly cheated by the smooth talking brokers, insurance salesmen and financial advisors who listened intently as they told them their hopes and dreams for the future and then sold them any old crap that happened to pay the most commission.

*RARITY – **10***
With investments way down from their peaks and millions of investors looking with dread at their severely depleted investment portfolios few have been left untouched. It's a case of 'we're all in this together' apart from those that sold them in the first place who have long since spent the commission on a new holiday home on Cyprus.

? *WHAT ARE THEY DOING NOW?*
Passing through the five stages of grief – denial, anger, bargaining, depression and acceptance, although currently stuck at anger and not particularly looking forward to reaching the depression or acceptance stage. Shortly they will have to come to terms with the harsh reality of having had their dreams shat on once more, which brings back bitter childhood memories of when their father forced them into accounting instead of engaging their latent singing ability.

 AVOIDANCE | REVENGE STRATEGIES
1. Give up on the investment thing and just stick with putting what little money you have left at the end of the month into a low performing building society account or under the mattress. Paradoxically you will end up with a lot more money than anyone who has invested it in the markets.

2. Write a book called 'The Sins of Commission' which details the sorry tales of commission hungry financial services salespeople ripping off the naive investor. Include a few stock images of cheesy, sharp-suited salesmen sitting in the front room of a 75 year old granny demonstrating through a series of complex graphs how her money could double or indeed triple over the next 25 years.

3. Set up an investor's revenge shop which sells a variety of farm implements and assorted reconditioned weapons used for hand-to-hand combat in the trenches of the Western Front.

4. Move into law where you can probably make a lot of money off the back off the current wave of litigation. Specialise in anything which is investor related and offer a no-win, big-fee deal to your clients. They will be so irate that they will sign anything without reading the small print (some things never change).

5. Become a financial advisor and call your firm 'Lemon Investments' with the slogan 'never knowingly made a decent return'. Include lemons on your business card, website and brochures as this is essential to establishing a reliable and trusted brand.

THE IRATE INVESTOR:

☐ Can blame someone else for their predicament

☐ Only has them self to blame

☐ Deserves our sympathy and should be hugged

☐ Deserves our contempt and should be shot

The Living Big Loser

When I was newly married, my wife and I lived in a small maisonette, nothing fancy you understand but just enough for us to store what few possessions we had at the time. One evening, one of our friends came round with her new boyfriend. A nice chap as I recall but what caught our eye was the flash car he was driving – a BMW. We thought he must be doing incredibly well, especially as we had a clapped out old Renault at the time, replete with a dent in the side and the wheel arches rusting away. Looking back, it is easy to see why we were impressed, but the guy didn't own the car, he simply had an enormous loan the size of a small mortgage, barely enough to fund his ego never mind the – rapidly depreciating – car. But what this tells us of course is how easy it is to be bowled over by someone's flashy car. The same is true of their house, their ponies, and their rather nice lightweight mountain bike handmade from titanium with Guatemalan rubber tyres embossed with gold leaf. When someone has something fancy, like an Aston Martin DB9 for example, it leads to a sense of anxiety in the person that doesn't, causing them to do one of three things: take out a loan and blow £100000 on a similar car; feel very depressed and cry; take out their penknife and envy mark it. I prefer the third option as it is generally more satisfying. This is known as 'status anxiety' and it has a lot to answer for, including of course the mess we are now in, not to mention all the goddamn 'Chelsea Tractors' on the roads, driven by idiots who want to impress with their personalised number plates, (you know the sort, like AR53 1, KN013 and T1T H3AD).

It is well known that status anxiety, keeping up with the Joneses, or any other label you want to give it, causes all sorts of problems such as depression, addiction and an insatiable need to buy more 'stuff'. We also know that buying things does little for your self esteem; once you have spent a few grand on the latest stereo system, it just clutters up your front room and in any case five minutes later you want an even bigger one. This, for those of you who are interested, is known as the 'hedonic treadmill'; the more you have, the more you want. There is no doubt that over the years this has gotten decidedly worse as more and more people have been sucked into 'living big'. You can see it in the cars people drive, the McMansions and gated communities that despoil the greenbelt, and the increasing number of self-storage facilities – the ones you couldn't miss even in the fog with their gaudy orange exteriors and the queues of trailer-driving consumers choking up the roads with the next load of crap they don't need and have no room for. Much of this phenomenon has been greatly enabled by freely available credit, why bother saving up for anything tomorrow, when you can have it today?

Those who decided that living big was for them went on a massive spending binge buying whatever they could to make them look better than their neighbours – the bigger house, the huge conservatory, the yacht, the lama and of course the trampoline,

(needed in order to see over the neighbour's fence and assess their net worth). There was no stopping them, and as the credit kept flowing they felt that they could enjoy the lifestyle with no downside. Times were good and it didn't matter a hoot what your income was, because nobody cared; the banks didn't; the credit card companies didn't and the local loan shark certainly didn't care. So if you needed a mortgage that was 500 times you annual income – no problem, and if you really wanted to spend £4000 on a cherished number plate to match you new car then why not, you deserved it – you worked hard for a living and were a tosser.

However, as the Credit Crunch took hold those who had been living big found that their lifestyle came to an abrupt halt. No more credit and no more fun. When the music stopped it was patently obvious to anyone with a basic grasp of calculus that those who were living big were in fact big losers, and justifiably so. No longer able to service their debts, they have been desperately 'deleveraging' (the economic term for getting rid of as much of your debt as possible, or ideally offloading it onto an unsuspecting idiot, like the government for example). Recognising that they can no longer use their houses as piggybanks or play the monthly merry-go-round with their credit card debt, they have been selling up anything they can on eBay at rock bottom prices. They have also been losing their loved ones, who finally saw through all the jewellery and presents and high living, and realised that their spouse was an arsehole devoid of personality, and was in fact no good in bed either.

☐ Tick here when you have spotted the Living Big Loser

SYMPATHY RATING – 2
The Living Big Loser deserves everything they get, as they can only blame themselves for the mess they find themselves in. They took a leaf out of Gordon Brown's little book of economic success and spent like crazy, expecting the good times to roll on forever. They like to complain and bitch that it is unfair and they had no choice but to buy an eight bedroomed house in the country and a top of the range Land Rover. I'm sorry, but you didn't need any of this at all. The only reason you bought it all was because you were empty inside and believed that having loads of stuff or a big house would somehow make you feel good about yourself and win you lots of friends. As you now know, that isn't the case; you hate yourself and so do they, so deal with it.

RARITY – 6
The Living Big Loser is pretty common these days and not just restricted to our poor banking friends and former Masters of the Universe who have been kicked out of their jobs or who have now joined the ever expanding ranks of the civil service. They are coming from all walks of life with the common factor being their access to easy credit and a desire to be like Madonna or the Beckhams.

WHAT ARE THEY DOING NOW?

Waking up screaming every night covered in sweat and wondering how on earth they are ever going to pay back all the money they have borrowed. In their more lucid moments they can be found running around their enormous 'McMansions' looking for the tranquilisers they misplaced, considering taking an overdose.

AVOIDANCE | REVENGE STRATEGIES

1. Always live within your means and avoid falling into the trap of trying to outdo your neighbours. It is far better to save your money and spend it wisely.

2. Sit down with them and explain to them how to prepare a simple budget. Ask them to list their income and outgoings and challenge them on those items which seem frivolous, like mooring fees or their monthly subscription to the lap dancing club.

3. Perform a simple experiment on them. Place two sweeties on a table and ask them to sit down facing them. Then, tell them that if they *don't* immediately grab them and push them into their mouth, you will give them two more. Naturally, when they can't wait you can tell them that they will never be truly successful and in fact will most likely contract Type two diabetes.

4. Suggest they go on 'Life Laundry' where they can find out what the root cause is of their obsession with living big and spending way beyond their means. It will probably turn out to be something quite simple, like everyone thinks they are a tosser.

5. Set up a self-help group for Living Big Losers where they can sit around in a semicircle and tell their tales of debt and woe whilst crying into crumpled up credit card slips.

THE LIVING BIG LOSER:

☐ Can blame someone else for their predicament

☐ Only has them self to blame

☐ Deserves our sympathy and should be hugged

☐ Deserves our contempt and should be shot

The Low-Bonus Banker

The one thing you have to remember about our dear banking friends is that they are only interested in one thing and that's their bonus; nothing more and nothing less. Just ask their wives and mistresses – unless there is money involved, they just can't seem to get it up. As one of the idiots on 'The Apprentice' said, 'Making money is better than sex'. Whilst on the subject of 'The Apprentice', if they are the cream of what the UK has to offer, then we are indeed doomed; most of them aren't even capable of cleaning a toilet, let alone becoming multimillionaire business men or women. I think 'The Tosser' would be a far more apt name for the show, because it's usually the biggest tosser that usually wins. I am, of course getting ahead of myself.

It has been scientifically and statistically proven that most bankers do no more than two months work a year. The remaining ten is split evenly between worrying about how much 'bonuuuuuuuuuuuuus' (yes, if you listen to any banker they actually pronounce bonus in this way; in fact, the bigger the bonus, the longer the intonation will go on for) they are going to receive and fretting about how they will spend it. Do they go for the top of the range Land Rover this year, or an apartment on the Baltic Sea? It is a sad fact, but this really matters to them. They will of course tell you that they love their job (which is a lie) and that they care about what they do with their clients' money (another porky) and that they can more than justify their multimillion and even billion dollar salaries (another untruth, I'm afraid). I knew one investment manager who looked after the pensions of major companies who told me that he was more than happy to gamble with the money because it wasn't his and who cared if he lost it; well apart from a few thousand pensioners, I guess no one. He also told me that he was unwilling to invest his own cash in the same way. Kind of sums up the entire industry doesn't it?

The bankers thought they were better than everyone else. School kids and university graduates everywhere would make a beeline for a career in the city where they could learn about all the exciting ways to make money out of thin air. They became experts in collateralised debt, exotic trades, futures, swaps, options, and all manner of things which made them look cool amongst their friends. But the one thing they loved to do was to tell everybody how big it was (their bonus of course). Over the years bankers came to depend on their bonus to pay for their houses, fleets of sports cars and a celebrity lifestyle. Whole industries sprung up around them seeking to get a piece of the action: 'bottom-feeders', is their technical term I believe. These included butlers, cleaners, toilet flushers, personal trainers, house sitters, pet managers, dog walkers and other assorted personal services, like masseuses which came with extras. The bankers were too busy making money to deal with trivial things such as ironing their silk underpants.

Of course, now that the house of cards has come crashing down, and the banks have been nationalised, the poor banker has lost their only sense of self worth. They have

become the worst possible thing – The Low Bonus Banker. With no friends, low self esteem, unable to pay their mortgage, and with their wives and mistresses leaving them for the increasingly better paid civil servant, the banker is feeling down in the dumps. Feeling hard done by and unappreciated by Mr and Mrs Average who have lost everything, they are suffering from a crisis of confidence, depression, stress and addiction related issues (drink, drugs, casual sex, internet dating, etc.). Good business for the rehab clinics and psychotherapists, which goes to show that not everyone does badly in a recession. Their problems have been compounded by politicians seeking to impose punitive taxes on their bonuses and anarchists and pensioners baying for their blood and suggesting they commit suicide or be hung from lampposts. Bashing a Banker is in season and will be for quite some time. And as for the bottom-feeders, they are experiencing the bottom falling out of their world too. Perhaps they can now get a proper job, if indeed there are any left.

☐ Tick here when you have spotted the Low Bonus Banker

SYMPATHY RATING – 0
No one cares about the Low Bonus Banker and in fact most people would rather they just buggered off. They have had it so good for so many years; all their complaining falls on deaf ears and is incredibly annoying. If they were stupid enough to spend all their millions on pointless goods, mistresses and overblown mortgages, that's their problem, not ours. Had they been sensible (surely anyone who wears red braces who isn't a skinhead or a member of a far right wing party must be an idiot) and saved most of their money they could be living the life of Riley for the rest of their natural lives. But we all know that the majority didn't. Sympathy also wears thin when it was their reckless behaviour that got us into this mess in the first place. Plus of course, we actually own the banks these days – so much for free market economics.

RARITY – 10
The Low Bonus Banker is easy to spot. With tens of thousands of bankers on the street, and those who are left in work worrying about how little bonus they will be getting, you can see them talking earnestly to anyone that will listen, spewing forth their tales of woe rather like the Ancient Mariner. As the recession continues to takes its toll and as more banks are nationalised we should expect to see many more Low Bonus Bankers bitching about how tiny their incomes are (but still well in excess of £250000)

WHAT ARE THEY DOING NOW?
For those still in employment, they will be putting in even longer hours to try and impress their equally desperate boss in order to avoid the next swing of the axe. For those who have sunk even lower, you will find them serving you

your special fried rice with crispy noodles for a paltry tip (but at least they will be impeccably dressed). Some are on the fast track to becoming teachers which is the latest ruse by the government to ensure that no one who comes out of the schooling system has an IQ greater than an amoeba. Maybe they will be able to help the next generation employ complex hedging strategies to simple arithmetic, or how to pronounce 'bonuuuuuuuuuuuuus' properly.

AVOIDANCE | REVENGE STRATEGIES

1. Don't associate with Low Bonus Bankers they are insufferable bores with small genitals. In fact I would advise that you don't associate with bankers at all, they will cramp your style.

2. If you can no longer aspire to becoming a grossly overpaid banker, why not join the Civil Service, where you can still get bonuses even if you cock everything up … a bit like the bankers then.

3. Point them in the direction of JK Galbraith's excellent book 'The Economics of Innocent Fraud' which suggests that big pay settlements are little more than grand larceny, legitimised by the pretence that they were subject to shareholder, auditor and regulator oversight.

4. The next time they complain about their bonus, remind them that you are in fact their boss given that you own the bank along with the rest of us and tell them they are fired.

5. Offer them some warmed up beef burgers instead of their annual bonus. When they complain tell them how lucky they are not to be starving.

THE LOW BONUS BANKER:

☐ Can blame someone else for their predicament

☐ Only has them self to blame

☐ Deserves our sympathy and should be hugged

☐ Deserves our contempt and should be shot

The Miserable Middle Class

For a long, long time, people across the world have aspired to be become middle class. Recognising they would never be, or indeed want to be, *upper* class with all that inbreeding and stupid voices, they wanted to prove to everyone that they had clawed their way out of the gutter without the benefit of mummy and daddy's trust fund. Equally, they wanted to be more than just a working class zero; poorly paid with a low life expectancy and forced to wear blue overalls at work, toiling under insufferable conditions for 27 hours a day. Being middle class was something special. It meant that you probably had a bit of cash left over at the end of the month to spend on a few luxury items like food for example; you had a relatively decent job which didn't involve getting your hands dirty; some reasonable and useful qualifications and lived in a house with more than one room and an inside toilet. You could hold your head up high and saunter down the street with a modicum of self-respect (unlike the working class who would still be working and the upper class who were too inbred to walk properly). Over time, the ranks of the middle classes have swelled as economies across the world have expanded and in some far flung places such as China, they now constitute more than 60% of the population.

Although it is great to be middle class, it comes with a whole bunch of issues which range from an incessant need to social climb, putting on unnecessary telephone voices when speaking to the vicar, through to struggling to prove to everyone else that you are more middle class than they are. And with this comes the non-stop boasting about how good they are, how much money they have, and how it is so important to give charity to the millions of poor people in the world; it's what makes the middle class, well, middle class. All this came at a cost and for some a significant one, as in order to compete against the rest of the middle class, families around the world have been on a non-stop spending fest. Such spending has included sending their precious children off to private school (to enable the seeds of their loins to get a few extra GCSEs); buying horses which their precocious, opinionated and slightly obese daughter rides occasionally; hiring servants so that they didn't ever have to lift a finger doing menial work again; and purchasing a clutch of overseas properties so that they can send ego-boasting Christmas cards to their 'friends' with strap lines like *'Happy Christmas from the Smith Family – London, Norfolk, Gdansk and Lagos'* replete with cheesy images of them outside each of their properties holding glasses of champagne. The spiral of competition sucked in millions of middle class mugs all desperate to set themselves apart from everyone else. For a while it seemed to work.

Since the Credit Crunch, however, the middle classes have refocused their angst on moaning about the parlous state of the economy and their personal finances. Indeed, these days being middle class is a bit crap. If you are upper class you may have lost a few billion, but it is unlikely that you will end up on Queer Street anytime soon. Plus,

of course, you can offset your investment losses against your future income so that you never have to pay tax again. If you happen to be in the working classes, most of your income is from government handouts anyway and like the upper classes you pay little or no tax. So unless you have been silly and overspent on your credit cards (in an attempt to emulate the middle classes no doubt), then, equally, you are fine. Because the middle class is the only stratum of the population that is capable of paying any tax, they are getting hammered by tax hikes and price increases on absolutely everything. As a result, their carefully constructed world now resembles a multiple pileup on the M6. The private school fees are now unaffordable so little Jonny is having to go back to state school where he will most probably end up with fewer GCSEs and a few black eyes, but perhaps a little bit more socially adept and less arrogant; the horses are having their brains blown out and are being sold to be mashed up and made into glue; the servants are being 'let go'; and poor mummy and daddy are having to learn how to clean toilets and cook again. All the houses which they loved to boast about are in the process of being sold at a loss or repossessed by overzealous bankers desperate to liquidate their losses. Tough times ahead no doubt, but it will be nice to see the end of the insatiable name dropping, boasting and generally dull conversation that have presided over the past decade or more. Perhaps now the middle classes will begin to discuss the important issues of the day, such as war with Iran, that crazy midget Kim Jong IL, 'Life on Mars', and whether or not Ken in 'Coronation Street' will ever shag Deirdre again.

☐ **Tick here when you have spotted the Miserable Middleclass**

SYMPATHY RATING – **6**
The middle classes are somewhat buggered, all things considered. Stuck in the middle of the social spectrum as they are, they will never get any support from the government and they have insufficient assets to ride out the downturn. As their world comes tumbling down, they are turning increasingly to drink, drugs and casual sex to dull the bitter disappointment and loss of self esteem. Still, on a positive note, by the time they have been taxed to death and forced back down to the working class, they will at least get a few state handouts.

RARITY – **7**
With so many people claiming to be middle class we should expect to see plenty of the Miserable Middle Class over the coming months and possibly years (after all, taxes won't be coming back down in our lifetime). You can spot them looking glum around shopping centres with the Pound Shop bag carefully concealed inside a Marks and Spencer 'bag for life'. Only their pallid complexion gives away the loss of their Florida holiday home; it's back to camping on waterlogged Scottish moorlands, sharing communal showers with the rest of the great unwashed.

WHAT ARE THEY DOING NOW?

Trying to explain to their family and friends that they never bought into the whole middle class bullshit in the first place and that it is a liberating experience for little Jonny to have the shit kicked out of him every morning in the school playground by a couple of council estate thugs. And when it's all over, booking a holiday to Turkey at 84 pence per person; you can't go wrong at that price, can you?

AVOIDANCE | REVENGE STRATEGIES

1. Steer clear of all of the typical middle class haunts and avoid eye contact with anyone you suspect might be middle class. Trust me, you will feel better about yourself.

2. Pretend to be a fully paid up member of the classless society and when asked, claim to be living a nomadic existence.

3. Write your memoir about how miserable it is to be middle class and get it endorsed by Oprah Winfrey. You will need to include some kind of physical abuse like your parents beating you until you agreed to go to private school, as that's the only thing people like to read about these days.

4. Join one of the many demonstrations run by the Miserable Middle Class to protest at how unfair it is to be saddled with massive amounts of debt by the incompetent and irresponsible government. If you are lucky you might get beaten up during the ensuing riot and be able to make some cash through the courts.

5. Buy them the 'My Little Pony Abattoir Set' in which they can relive the final moments of their beloved pony. In parallel, why not consider starting a horse-glue service (with the brand name 'Equine Strength') in which you emboss pots of glue with pictures of their horse. Although no longer with them, they can at least enjoy making use of their sturdy steed's by-product when making a collage depicting their family's fall from grace.

THE MISERABLE MIDDLE CLASS:

☐ Can blame someone else for their predicament

☐ Only has them self to blame

☐ Deserves our sympathy and should be hugged

☐ Deserves our contempt and should be shot

The Newly Liberated

During World War Two when most of Europe was under the Nazi Jackboot, local populations suffered terrible deprivations for many years. So when the Allied troops pushed the Germans back to the Rhine they were ecstatic that they had at last been liberated.

According to the Press, similar levels of elation are being felt across the world as workers are shed from companies as fast as the Allies rolled up the German Army in 1945. Having suffered years of deprivation, working under insufferable conditions workers are beside themselves that they are being given the opportunity to take their enthusiasm elsewhere. Having for years turned up at the same time and location, doing the same mind numbing work in the accounts department day after day, their souls destroyed and creative juices dried up, being made redundant was the kick up the backside they needed to finally go and pursue their lifelong ambition to become a street artist or glass blower.

Newspapers are full of the Newly Liberated extolling the virtues of their new found freedom away from the corporate handcuffs and bullshit that ruled their lives for what seemed like an eternity. Now free from the tyranny of the working day, they can walk around their houses semi-naked, turn their hand to a bit of pottery and continue with their online gambling addiction comfortable in the knowledge that they are no longer doing it on company time.

Those not interested in going straight back into the work thing often choose to go back to school or university to pick up where they left off with their studies or perhaps gain a new qualification. Enrolments have leapt as the Newly Liberated go back to being students once more. Naturally it won't be quite the same this time around as you will be considerably older, and when you are walking around the library all the nubile young students will think you are either some kind of pervert, or a lonely post grad without friends. The good news is that you will get the chance to learn to read something other than a tabloid newspaper every day, remind yourself just how bad some lecturers really are and be moaned at by your spouse that all you ever do is work. Apart from going for the obvious qualifications associated with green technology – apparently the only part of economy which will be functioning five years from now – a favourite of the many so-called white collar workers who have been shown the door, is the MBA (Master of Business Administration – doesn't it sound dull?). Here you can learn what all that gobbledygook spouted by your CEO and the highly paid strategy consultants that swarmed all over the company like locusts actually meant. And eventually you might come to understand that it was mostly executives with MBAs that got us into this mess in the first place.

And of course for those who can't be bothered to find a new job (mainly because there aren't any) or who can no longer read or write properly, there is always the 'grown-up

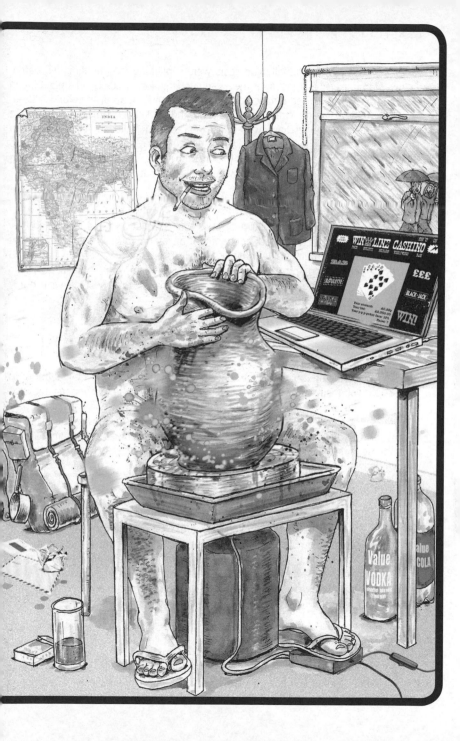

gap year'. Although traditionally gap years were something that students did before they went to university, or just after they graduated, the Newly Liberated are getting in on the game. With their redundancy cheque in hand and a map of the world laid out before them they sit like excited 19 year olds around the kitchen table debating where they will go. And once they have agreed that the Peshawar Valley in northern Pakistan sounds good, they will pack a rucksack, book their one-way ticket and kiss goodbye to doom and gloom Britain. And in a few months time they will send home a picture of themselves sharing some cow's blood with a Taliban scouting party.

Once the initial joy of escaping the rat race has died down however, the Newly Liberated come to the dawning realisation that what little money they received, or what little is left after paying off all their debts, will soon run out and that in the end they will have no choice but to go back and work for a crap organisation once more. What they also realise is that unless they have used their time wisely (i.e. not walking around their house semi-naked and gambling online) they will end up in an even worse job than before. So if you thought Accounts was bad, try spending the next five years doing balance sheet reconciliations; you will go insane.

☐ **Tick here when you have spotted the Newly Liberated**

SYMPATHY RATING – 2
Having the opportunity to pursue a lifelong ambition or think about what you really want to do with your life and perhaps finally understand what you are good at (something most companies just don't care about) is a good thing. The Newly Liberated are a lucky bunch; well those that have enough money to do what they want. For those who have been liberated only to find themselves on the scrap heap then things won't be quite as much fun and they, of course, deserve all our sympathy.

RARITY – 9
With unemployment creeping up around the world – 2 million in the UK, 6 million in the US and 200 million in China, the world is swarming with the Newly Liberated. You can spot them wearing thick reading glasses and poring over 'The Art of Forensic Accounting' at the local library (so that you recognise that they are students and not some sad loser who just likes accountancy), or hitchhiking in flip-flops along the eastern seaboard of Australia looking tired, worn out and covered in dust because they have run out of cash.

WHAT ARE THEY DOING NOW?
In a general state of despair as the tiny moment of freedom they enjoyed during which they were spared the daily grind is finally coming to an end. Rather like the feeling you got as a kid when the summer holidays were nearing an end and you had to go back to school, the poor sods turn in only after having downed

a bottle of vodka to deaden the pain and set their alarm clocks for 6:00 am once more. Still, with any luck they will get made redundant again in a year or two and they can do it all over again.

 AVOIDANCE | REVENGE STRATEGIES
1. If you are still in work and wishing that you weren't, then I would strongly advise that you avoid the Newly Liberated at all costs as you will find their conversations about how it's saved them and given them the one chance they always craved both nauseating and very annoying.

2. Get a group of your friends to dress up in German Army uniforms and hunt down the Newly Liberated and when you have rounded them up take them back to their employers.

3. Offer a blogging service in which the Newly Liberated can record their inner thoughts as they go through the experience of being sacked, thinking about their future, what they studied today, how their new business venture is faring and what colour their poo was this morning when they woke up in the Gobi desert.

4. If you happen to be on holiday somewhere and you spot a flip-flop wearing Newly Liberated middle aged couple, offer them a lift. During the journey describe in detail the five star resort you're staying at and then dump them miles from anywhere. As you push them out of the car, tell them to get a job.

5. Set up a new religious sect that claims that money and greed has wrought the wrath of Gaia and aim it at the Newly Liberated. Offer them peace and harmony and renewed hope in the milk of human kindness. Set up your sect in a few square miles of freshly cleared Brazilian rainforest and ask that those who enter give up all their worldly possessions and especially their cash. Make sure that you have plenty of excuses to be away from the compound (promoting the new sect for example) so that you can enjoy all inclusive holidays in the Caribbean.

THE NEWLY LIBERATED:

☐ Can blame someone else for their predicament

☐ Only has them self to blame

☐ Deserves our sympathy and should be hugged

☐ Deserves our contempt and should be shot

The No Responsibility Regulator

It is well known that without some kind of regulation the corporate and financial markets would be a total disaster as companies and investment firms would rip people off, spend money unwisely and use it to enrich themselves rather than their investors. Now that kind of thing may have happened in the past, as it did at the time of the South Sea Bubble, and following the Dotcom boom when all that nasty accounting fraud perpetrated by the likes of Enron and WorldCom took place, but surely that wouldn't happen in today's well managed financial system? Indeed, after the financial scandals of the early years of the millennium, the clever Americans voted in the Sarbanes Oxley Act in which the CFOs of public companies were required to sign off their annual accounts in blood (yes, literally their own blood; it's in the small print if you look carefully enough). And if it turned out they were liars they would find themselves in a tiny prison cell with the partner from their auditing firm sporting orange jumpsuits and chains. This was rather like bolting the door after the horse had bolted, incarcerating a few of the higher profile criminals so that we could go back to business as usual, comfortable in the knowledge that the rights had been wronged and everyone could be trusted again. There were even annual events where the most trusted companies would be awarded for their good behaviour. The CEO of the most trusted firm would be cheered by their peers, regulators and politicians as they received their Golden Halo Award. And, just like the Oscars, those attending would be provided with a goody bag full of exciting gifts such as a few thousand share options from the winning company.

So, having cleaned out all the bad eggs from the corporate world, the regulators could pat themselves on the back and relax knowing it was a job well done. Well, not quite it seemed. Having sorted out the corrupt CEOs and CFOs, it was now the banks' turn to be a tad naughty and get away with some very dodgy practices. Practices like building up a tsunami of toxic debt by packaging up poor performing loans and selling them off to innocent investors; paying eye watering bonuses to the dice rollers who manned the front office; and choosing to ignore (well actually sack) anyone who thought that what they were doing was just plain wrong. Even when such reckless actions were brought to the attention of the regulators they dismissed the whistleblowers out of hand as being alarmist, childish or just plain jealous and continued to have cosy dinners with the bosses of the banks who were setting up the whole capitalist system to fail.

True to form of course, the No Responsibility Regulator mobilised only when everything had gone completely to rat shit. Only then did they feel suitably emboldened and started to flex their regulatory muscles by telling the bankers that they had been very naughty and they really ought to put their house in order. Taking no responsibility at all for their role in failing to properly regulate anything (apart from perhaps their breathing), they

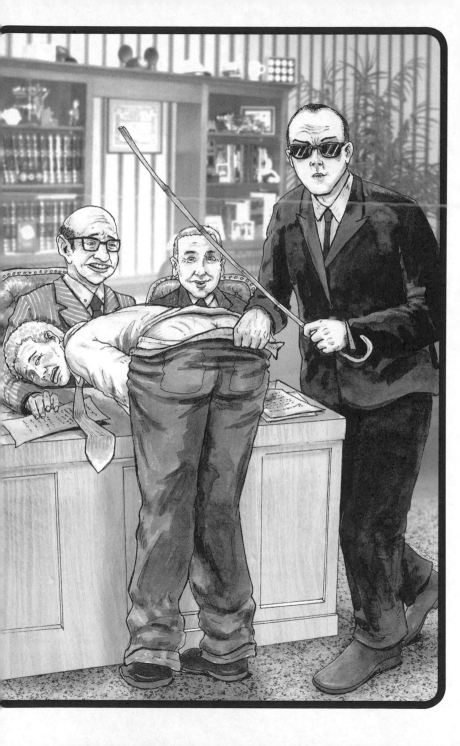

got onto their high horse and started bolting all the stable doors once more. This was accompanied by bold statements such as 'we will ensure that the financial system never, ever, drags down the economy again', 'We will change the game; this is not about moving deckchairs around on the Titanic, we will actually paint them first' and 'We will make you very frightened of us by dressing up as Orcs and brandishing plastic swords'. Fine words indeed, but we all know that even when they do try to change things, the lobbyists (i.e. those who are going to be regulated to death) will scupper any useful changes so that the new regulation ends up requiring the banks, hedge funds and insurance companies to make sweeping changes like using blue letterheads on their official communications.

Then there are the non-executive directors, the smart and experienced operators drawn from the great and the good who are employed to keep the reckless CEOs in check. Their role is simple, make sure the company is run well, follows all the rules and ensure things don't get out of hand by paying too much money for piss poor results. All well and good until you realise that they all sit on each other's board of directors and vote themselves pay rises every year. And whenever there is any questionable behaviour or when the CEO could do with a bit of extra cash, the non execs cough a bit, rustle their papers and agree to whatever the CEO wants. Naturally they know that when it's their turn to ask for what they need the favour will be reciprocated.

But what really sticks in the craw is when bankers who have *earned* hundreds of millions of dollars suggest that compensation has got out of hand and needs to be reined in. It's like Guy Fawkes recommending that gunpowder needs to be regulated to stop people like him from attempting to blow up Parliament.

☐ **Tick here when you have spotted the No Responsibility Regulator**

SYMPATHY RATING – **0**

If I am not mistaken, the regulators are government run bodies and are therefore meant to be working on our behalf. So surely they should be watching out for us and working hard to stop CEOs, bankers and others who are at the table of the casino economy from screwing it all up? Maybe it's just too complex for them or they can't be bothered, but there can be no sympathy for them when they state that they didn't see it coming.

RARITY – **10**

It is very difficult to spot a regulator who seems to be up to the job, in fact it is highly likely that whenever you lift the occasional rock you will find the No Responsibility Regulator cowering beneath it. Because they are normally timid creatures you have to be eagle-eyed to see them. However, the one time you will see them is when the economy has gone to rack and ruin and they pretend they are hard by clenching their fists and holding their breath so that they go red in the face.

WHAT ARE THEY DOING NOW?
Sitting in their offices debating how they will introduce the cane into the regulation process and then practicing their technique on a lowly administration assistant.

AVOIDANCE | REVENGE STRATEGIES
1. Recognise that the corporate and financial systems are highly complex and imperfect and hence it will be virtually impossible to ever regulate them properly.

2. Consider joining a board of directors as a non-executive director. It's an easy job with great perks and you will never be held accountable for anything you do.

3. Design and market Regulatory Canes. In addition to holding master classes on how to cane effectively, ensure you use only the best materials made locally from renewable sources.

4. Establish a new and powerful regulator who has the power to inflict capital punishment on those who broke the rules. A bit harsh perhaps, but you won't see many reckless CEOs and bankers after the first clutch have been brutally dispatched.

5. Employ Sir David Attenborough to start a new television series called 'In Search of Rare Regulators'. Follow him as he rummages through the wreckage of the economy searching for non-vertebrate regulators.

THE NO RESPONSIBILITY REGULATOR:

☐ Can blame someone else for their predicament

☐ Only has them self to blame

☐ Deserves our sympathy and should be hugged

☐ Deserves our contempt and should be shot

The Not Quite Such a Master of the Universe

There have always been three career choices that have been considered to be much better than many others; banking, consultancy and law. Sure, becoming a florist and selling flowers is a nice thing to do, but it rarely cuts any mustard when at dinner parties or when you are trying to pick up someone of the opposite sex.

People who followed such career paths considered themselves to be the Masters of the Universe; the all powerful movers and shakers who would advise corporations and governments around the world, mainly it has to be said on how best to part with their cash, (as their fees were always extortionately high and most of the advice eventually discarded). The Master of the Universe was king of the hill; working long hours and selling their soul to their employers but getting a nice pile in the process. They were easily spotted by their arrogant swagger, bespoke suits, hand-made shoes and double-cuffed shirts with no pockets; if they needed a pen they would just take it from their client. Outside work they would insist on wearing pink Ralph Lauren cardigans draped around their shoulders with Oakley sunglasses pushed up into their expertly coiffured hairdos. I guess they thought it made them look cool. These were the people who kept whole sectors of the economy alive such as the champagne industry, over-priced celebrity chef restaurants, the corporate entertaining sector and the airlines that depended on their business class travel to keep profit margins high. Like the government, they could spend freely confident in the knowledge that it wasn't their money and that the wonderful junkets they all attended could be charged back to their clients, (although unlike politicians, porn films were completely out of the question). Fashion magazines would run competitions on the best dressed professionals from these firms which did nothing for their image, making them look overly effeminate and ever so slightly stupid. Surely any self-respecting client would want to know why their highly paid advisors were attending a photo shoot in Mayfair instead of completing that vitally important board presentation?

When times were good, the career choices of newly minted graduates was like a 'Who's Who' of professional services, names like Lehman Brothers, Bear Sterns, AIG, Ernst & Young, Slaughter and May and other high-end legal firms, consultancies and investment banks. When asked what they wanted to do, every undergraduate, yes even those who were studying 13th Century English Literature with Urdu and Social Anthropology, would get awfully excited when they told you that they were joining Merrill Lynch. Not because they had any real interest in banking, law or consultancy, but because they knew they would make a skip load of cash quickly and would be the envy of all their friends. Those who weren't employed by such firms (and who ended up as their clients) generally hated them. But as always with these things, they felt compelled to use them

because at least half a dozen of their employees actually knew something useful and weren't complete tossers who shouted a lot.

As the boom times continued the rank and file of the Masters of the Universe ballooned as the companies which employed them expanded to meet the need set by the whirlwind of mergers and acquisitions, court cases associated with failed consultancy assignments, and the divorces of the partners and senior executives. Times were good and as expansion continued the firms began to scrape the barrel of talent, recruiting anyone who could spell 'money' or who could take someone's watch and use it to tell the time. The Masters of the Universe strutted their stuff in restaurants and bars across the country leaving big tips to the poorly paid waiter who was expected to clear up after their chimps' tea party, or for the well-endowed, mini-skirted barmaid who knew how to milk them for everything they had in their wallet. But in reality, they were a lonely bunch whose only true friend was the fellow professional they happened to be shagging at the time, or the lap dancer who was gyrating over their groin.

As the economy has tanked so has the source of their wealth and their prospects now don't look quite as rosy as they once did. In fact, the Not Quite Such a Master of the Universe is far less confident than they used to be and their arrogant swagger has been replaced by a down at heel shuffle as thousands are being given the cabman's farewell. Graduates too are now turning to other careers. Perhaps within the charity sector where they can attend to the needs of the former masters of the universe who are in desperate need of support now that their bubbles of invincibility have burst. Plus of course, they realise that being a banker, lawyer or consultant these days is liable to get you beaten up. For those that remain, the fun times are over; no more jolly days out where you drink as much champagne as you can; no more business class flights (it's the back of the aircraft with the rest of the prols) and forget about staying at five star hotels, it's the Holiday Inn for you. They all look rather comical as they turn up in their sports cars at rundown hotels on the edge of industrial estates, or snake down the aisle of a 747 only to end up sitting next to an obese gentleman in row 45 for eight hours. It does wonders for the hand-woven suit.

☐ **Tick here when you have spotted the Not So Quite Master of the Universe**

*SYMPATHY RATING – **1***
I don't think there is anyone in the world right now who has much sympathy for the Not Quite Such a Master of the Universe. In fact I would say that there a lot of people who would gladly punch their lights out. That said they are perhaps looked on more sympathetically than politicians, so they ought to be thankful for that.

*RARITY – **7***
Given that lawyers, consultants and bankers were breeding like rabbits during the boom times, it should come as no surprise that the Not Quite Such a Master of the Universe is very common. Even those out of work still have a habit of wearing pink sweaters draped over the shoulders; it's a dead giveaway.

WHAT ARE THEY DOING NOW?

Contemplating the collapse of their career and wondering why they had wasted the best years of their life working 1000 hours a week for what constituted an empty existence. For those with a weaker disposition, they will be crying during their gestalt therapy sessions as the therapist investigates their relationship with their alcoholic mother. Others will be busy justifying that they really wanted to be a secondary school teacher after all, and that trying to get a bunch of feckless youths to understand the concept of simple arithmetic is far better than jetting off to Bermuda to close a deal with a reinsurance company. But whatever they are doing, they will still be stealing everyone's pens.

AVOIDANCE | REVENGE STRATEGIES

1. Understand that in life you are better off pursuing a worthwhile and rewarding career looking after the poor, needy and infirm. You may not earn as much, but you will have a better work-life balance, you will have more friends and everyone won't think that you're an arrogant arsehole.

2. Recommend that they see one of the government's 3600-strong army of new therapists who are there to deal with the current anxiety epidemic (good to see that the government continues to spend our taxes wisely).

3. Pose as a style guru and offer to do a fashion shoot with a number of professional firms. When you have finished doctor the image to make them all look like down-and-outs, and upload it to You Tube with the caption 'The Masters of the Hobo look'.

4. Set up a cut-price multi-services professional firm offering everything really cheaply – you might even persuade Stelios to back it ('Easy Law', 'Easy Consulting' 'Easy Fleecing'). You will be able to employ many of the ex-bankers, consultants and lawyers, at much reduced rates, and make yourself plenty of cash. For good measure make them all wear shiny suits, shirts with pockets and buy their own pens.

5. Design a Master of the Universe outfit and market it as an ego-enhancing product to banks, law firms and consultancies. Claim that wearing it improves productivity and makes the staff look cool. Ensure it is colourful and caters for the specific needs of each client – for example having a really big watch for the consultants, a pair of Day-Glo braces for the bankers and a handy guide to cynicism for the lawyers.

THE NOT SO QUITE MASTER OF THE UNIVERSE:

☐ Can blame someone else for their predicament

☐ Only has them self to blame

☐ Deserves our sympathy ad should be hugged

☐ Deserves our contempt and should be shot

The Nuevo Altruist

One of the core tenets of altruism is that the people who have this character trait never expect much in return, which is just as well I guess because they don't get paid much. It's great to see public-spirited people scooping up the mess from other people's dogs who poo with abandon on our streets and cities. They are lovely people and should be commended and even awarded for their behaviour. The same can be said of those who man the Samaritans' phone lines as one can only imagine that these are red hot right now with all the doom and gloom descending on us from a great height. I wonder what they do when they hear a former investment banker blubbing down the phone telling them that their wife has left them and their world is falling apart? If it was me, I would tell them exactly what I thought – that the world would be a much better place without them and no one would actually miss them that much (probably assuming they had been posted to the trading floor of the Mumbai stock exchange). And if it happened to be a down on their luck former-politician (who stood down for their outrageous expense claims) I would probably go round and despatch them myself. So I guess that's why I am not manning the phone lines and nice stable altruistic people are. There is an important lesson in this. Those that work in the charity sector; the genuine altruists, do so because they are wired differently from everyone else which makes the current trend for Nuevo Altruism all the more worrying.

When the economy was booming most people couldn't give a monkey's toss about anyone but themselves; that was Blair's Britain, his classless society that had no class. People would barely say hello to their neighbours, let alone go and help someone who had just collapsed in the street. Even where they did offer their support they would either be set upon by a bunch of knife-wielding youths or end up on a GBH charge because they'd helped a young lady to her feet. Greed may have been good for their wallets, but it was bad for their souls. It's funny, now that unemployment is rising many previously self-centred citizens who would happily kick a tramp as they walked past seem to be having a 'road to Damascus' moment. Suddenly they seem to be realising that they don't really want to spend the rest of their lives working as a geologist in some remote East African desert, making millions as a commodity trader or taking abuse down the phone in an Irish call centre as they attempt to sell the latest technology product to someone with no income. Instead they now want to be kind to people; to take an interest in global issues and to feel joy once again. Pass the barf bag why don't you? One has to ask whether this load of old tosh is just a convenient smokescreen so that they can hold their head up high and pretend not to care as they tell everyone they have been sacked from their job. And if only to prove the point they will come out with such bullshit statements like 'it was the best thing that ever happened to me', 'I feel so much more fulfilled', and 'it's profoundly life-changing to be working outside the consumer driven paradigm and fight for the poor people in the world'. Yeah right, if you believe this then you are either on mind bending drugs or just plain simple.

So why the sudden 'epiphany'? Did God or perhaps Buddha appear to them one evening whilst they were relaxing in front of 'Eastenders', or was it a case of them soiling their pants when they realised their comfortable existence was about to go bye-bye? I would wager the latter, but then who knows or indeed cares? The Nuevo Altruist has all the characteristics of a born again Christian – they reject rampant consumerism, spurn traditional money-making careers, look down on people who spend unwisely and harp on about the plight of the poor, sick and lonely. Their friends and family think they might have suffered a mental breakdown and suggest that they should visit their doctor, but they foam at the mouth and storm off.

Of course, it is delightful that charities will have such talented individuals working for them; maybe this will mean that there will be fewer 'charity muggers' on the streets, bullying people into parting with what little cash they have left. I do worry though that this new-found altruism is bound to disappear as soon as the 'green shoots of recovery' turn into a field of golden corn. And when they do you'll hear a massive sucking noise as all those who rushed into the charity sector during the recession make a beeline for any job that pays them big bucks. As for being nice; that was just a 'phase', they are all bastards in the end and it won't be long before they will be barging past the charity muggers and putting buttons or cereal into the little charity envelopes that are pushed through their letterbox every other week. Old habits die hard.

☐ **Tick here when you have spotted the Nuevo Altruist**

SYMPATHY RATING – **3**
In these difficult times the charity sector will undoubtedly suffer and that's a shame. Fortunately there are those that still give as much as they can to good causes and the people that have always had a kind heart will continue to do their best for those less fortunate in society. But I struggle with the emergence of these trendy types who all of a sudden (and often after years of selling their services to the highest bidder) are inexorably drawn to the 'charideeeee' sector. I don't buy into it – it is merely a convenient port in the current economic storm.

RARITY – **8**
With so many white collar workers losing their jobs, the numbers of Nuevo Altruists will increase until there are more people working for charities than actually giving to them. Although given time, they will all no doubt disappear. I guess it is like a 'charity tide', it comes in and it goes out – and only then do you get to see who's not carrying a collection tin.

WHAT ARE THEY DOING NOW?
Organising the latest flash mob event in which a bunch of trendy young prats descend on Waterloo Station and dance to the latest Girls Aloud tune

whilst squirting water pistols at passing commuters in a pathetic attempt to raise awareness for Water Aid.

AVOIDANCE | REVENGE STRATEGIES

1. Anyone who is being genuinely altruistic at this time deserves our credit and their efforts should be praised and they should certainly not have the piss taken out of them.

2. Develop a short quiz which is capable of testing the Nuevo Altruist's true altruism. Offer this to the charity sector to help them filter out all the trendy charlatans who are only there because they didn't fancy working for the government (the employer of the last resort).

3. Seek some government or perhaps EU funding which will allow you to research the phenomenon known as 'the charity-tide'. When you have finished your research get it published in a few well placed international journals and present your results at global charity conferences.

4. Set up your own charity for lonely Truck Drivers. Build a website which contains images of the poor truck drivers looking lonely and sad as they park up for the night in some lay by. Ideally include a mission statement and use this to attract the Nuevo Altruists who are interested in important world issues such as this one.

5. Organise your own flash mob using Twitter to bring all the newly unemployed trendy workers together at your local swimming pool. Ask that they come with a heavy ball and chain securely fastened to their right ankle so that you can highlight the plight of Death Row prisoners in the United States. When everyone arrives get them to jump into the deep end of the pool.

THE NUEVO ALTRUIST:

☐ Can blame someone else for their predicament

☐ Only has them self to blame

☐ Deserves our sympathy and should be hugged

☐ Deserves our contempt and should be shot

The Organic Food Fly-by-night

The middle class expend inordinate amounts of energy looking for ways to outdo each other by boasting about the cars they drive; the jobs they do; the salaries they earn; the nannies and other staff they employ; the newspapers they read; the holidays they go on; the houses they own and how talented their children are. Over the last few years, the middle class has found a new battlefield on which to wage their social climbing war, and that's the food they eat. As well as doing their weekly shop at the most expensive supermarkets possible, because it shows they are moneyed, they immediately latch onto the organic farming and fair trade ethos as soon as they can. And once Prince Charles got onto the bandwagon, there was no stopping them. You'd hear them in the supermarket 'Oh, yes I am with Prince Charles on this one; it's sooooooooo important to ensure eggs are free range and that cows are given a hot chocolate before they retire for the evening'. At dinner parties, guests attempt to outdo each other on which organic farm they buy their produce from and how 'reassuringly expensive' the food is. Of course you can taste the difference when you know the cow has been lovingly strangled to death in a meadow instead of killed with an electric prod down the abattoir! They also like to discuss the horrors of world trade before fair trade, genetically modified food and how they would rather 'die' than eat anything that has been chemically altered. And so it goes on, and on, and on. Boasting about houses (which had already started to plummet) has been replaced by boasting about locally produced organic food. Who'd have thought it would come to this?

Keen to cash in, the supermarkets replaced scrapings from the abattoir floor with organically reared produce replete with photos of clean shaven farmers informing the consumer how they like to give hand relief to their animals. Naturally, even these farmers have been pressurised by the buyers of the large supermarkets to provide such produce at rock bottom prices so they still can't make a living, (but at least they can tell their friends they are famous). Then there's the gaggles of middle aged women nodding in agreement and pointing out pictures of Brazilian children carrying back-breaking 50 kilo sacks of fair trade coffee beans to a flatbed lorry a quarter of a mile away down a treacherous ravine. It must be good to know that only those who are educated and well read can buy this kind of produce. Poor people can buy 'own brand' goods, it suits their pockets, and in any case they couldn't possibly understand anything of the plight of Third World producer countries or the impact of globalisation.

Although the middle classes don't like to admit it, since the Credit Crunch they have begun to trade down and as part of this process they have abandoned both fair trade and organically produced food. Funny, now that their income is plummeting and they're feeling pain themselves, it's farewell to fair trade, and who cares whether the chickens

were reared on organically produced corn feed? I want cheap food and I want it now. Once again, in order to cash in, the supermarkets have re-stocked their shelves with mechanically recovered offal fashioned into multi-packs of sausages and burgers. The cheesy pictures of clean shaven farmers have been replaced by 'three for the price of one' offers; why pay more when you can get rubbish own brand food that tastes like cardboard?

The shoppers lap it up and try to hide that they are middle class and finding things a bit tough. One recent incident involved a woman in the queue at Lidl's, the cut price supermarket. Her mobile phone rang and she replied curtly, 'I can't talk right now I am in the queue at Sainsbury's'.

☐ **Tick here when you have spotted the Organic Food Fly-by-night**

SYMPATHY RATING – 4
The middle class are such bores when all things are considered. They waste so much energy trying to look better than their neighbours that they fail to enjoy life. If only they would lose some of their pretensions they would be much happier. But as we know this isn't going to happen. Still, we can watch with some amusement as they try to avoid eye contact with people when they are shuffling up and down the aisles of the cheaper supermarkets, steering clear of the ever-decreasing organic food section, looking carefully at the labels (for the price of course) and checking it off against their carefully prepared shopping list whilst keeping tabs on the cost with their pocket calculator.

RARITY – 8
The Organic Food Fly-by-night is increasingly common and you will see them at Iceland and Lidl, or with baskets full of supermarkets' own brand produce. As the Credit Crunch continues to takes its toll on the wallets of the middle classes you should expect to see a lot more, so keep your eyes peeled. You may of course already be one.

WHAT ARE THEY DOING NOW?
Jumping onto the 'grow your own' bandwagon and seriously considering bribing a local council official to get hold of one of the few remaining allotments that hasn't been snapped up. They believe that their organic food credentials will at last be restored and they will be able to announce at their dinner parties that love organic food so much they decided to produce their own.

AVOIDANCE | REVENGE STRATEGIES
1. Be a proud value shopper. It shows that you are a canny individual who won't pay inflated prices for fancy organically produced food anymore.

2. If you still have some spare cash always buy fair trade and organically produced food; ideally you should make a big song and dance when selecting your items so that the middle class mothers on the next (own brand, massively discounted) aisle feel ashamed.

3. Pose as an organic farmer down on your luck and write to Jamie Oliver saying you're thinking of starting a battery chicken farm and would he be interested in investing? Perhaps just a cheesy endorsement then, Jamie?

4. The next time you attend a dinner party make a point of telling everyone how good the quality the own brand label food is. Get really excited and wave you arms about and make a point of boasting about how much money you save. It won't be long before the rest of the guests are boasting about it too and will have found a new battlefield for their social climbing neurosis.

5. Prepare a short pamphlet which promotes your own organic produce, print a few hundred of them and secure them underneath the windscreen wipers of expensive looking cars in your local supermarket's car park. Sit back and wait for the organically minded shoppers to beat a path to your door.

THE ORGANIC FOOD FLY-BY-NIGHT:

☐ Can blame someone else for their predicament

☐ Only has them self to blame

☐ Deserves our sympathy and should be hugged

☐ Deserves our contempt and should be shot

The Out of Touch Politician

In England, whenever a king got too big for their boots or out of touch with the plight of their subjects they were usually either set upon and quietly dispatched in some remote castle away from prying eyes or overthrown by some scheming usurper in a set piece battle. And over the last 1000 years or so there have been quite a few: Harold bought it at the Battle of Hastings; William II was *'accidentally'* shot with an arrow by one of his knights whilst hunting in the New Forest; Arthur was murdered by his own uncle; Edward II's bottom was introduced to a red hot poker; Richard II, who got a tad too arrogant and self-centred, was starved to death; child murdering Richard III was killed at the battle of Bosworth; and Charles I was beheaded by those evil Parliamentarians led by Cromwell. They may have thought they were second only to God, but unfortunately for them not everyone was of the same mind. Today, kings and queens wield little or no power and tend to be more useful cutting ribbons and promoting trade than anything else. Still, at least they aren't carted off and despatched in any number of unseemly ways like they used to be.

In their place, we now have, of course, our elected officials; the politicians that wield power and spend the majority of their time bickering amongst themselves. And just like any new reigning monarch would tell the people what they wanted to hear and that everything will be different this time around, so the politicians do these days. Although elected 'by the people and for the people', it is surprising just how out of touch most politicians are. They claim to be concerned about what is going on with their constituents, but are actually much more interested in thumbing through the spring catalogue from John Lewis and selecting the new pearl white bathroom suite that will be installed in their parents' house courtesy of the taxpayer. Of course, when the economy is booming, no one really cares what the politicians do so long as they keep out of everyone's hair and don't do anything silly like sell off our gold reserves at rock bottom prices, or introduce a stealth tax on pensions. However, when the economy goes down the toilet, everyone expects them to do something other than just spew out platitudes, false hopes and bullshit. It is at such times that the Out of Touch Politician comes into their own, doing such things as:

- claiming to have seen the 'green shoots' of recovery when the country is going to hell in a hand cart;
- walking round factories which are on the brink of closure claiming that they have a bright future and making cheesy gestures in front of the cameras whilst pretending to know a bit about car maintenance;
- voting themselves significant pay rises whilst everyone else (well those not employed by the government of course) have to make do with pay cuts and the sack;
- stating that the UK is well placed to weather the downturn when it is obvious to everyone else in the whole world that this patently isn't the case;

- blaming everything on the Americans;
- increasing taxes and crafting other means of raising revenue even though thousands of businesses and individuals are going bankrupt;
- complaining that everyone is being too pessimistic and should cheer their bloody selves up.

The worst example of the Out of Touch Politician is of course when they are on the world stage trying to big themselves up at joint press conferences. They grin from ear to ear like they have some kind of intestinal problem and spew out nauseating statements about how wonderful the other leader is and that they stand united, 'shoulder to shoulder'. The problem is that they don't because they are different heights. And the smiles look as though it they're something you would find in your nephew's wedding album (which has long been tucked away and forgotten about).

It is a crying shame that the Out of Touch Politician cannot be dispatched in the same way we used to rid ourselves of our useless kings, but these days that kind of thing usually winds you up in jail. Still, at least we can give them a damn good kicking in the elections when they come. Perhaps it will be only then that they realise they are not as in touch with electorate as they thought they were. It's the political wilderness for them, or perhaps a few lucrative non-executive directorships.

☐ **Tick here when you have spotted the Out of Touch Politician**

SYMPATHY RATING – **0**
Apart from those who actually pay to be a member of a political party (which has to be tax deductible for it to make any sense, or at least have a peerage attached to it) no one likes political parties or indeed politicians. They claim that they are from and with the people, but in the end they only care about themselves and as such deserve no sympathy from Joe Public whatsoever. We suffer them because if we didn't we would have to live under a dictatorship where we wouldn't be allowed to do anything without some busybody official poking their nose in and telling us what we can and cannot do, (... and the difference is exactly?)

RARITY – **9**
The Out of Touch Politician is everywhere right now, as they deploy every cliché in their armoury to prove to the electorate that they are in touch and actually have their finger on the pulse of the country. They may well do, but their lack of medical training means that they haven't realised that there is in fact no pulse to be found where they've currently got their fingers stuck.

WHAT ARE THEY DOING NOW?
Riding round the country in their chauffeur driven limousine visiting failing businesses and factories telling them (with a concerned face of course),

that they will have some good news for them all soon, like business rates are going up 15%. When not on their road shows, they spend their quieter moments hoping that the electorate is both stupid and has a short-term memory problem so that they can get voted in for another term, leaving them ample time to finish the job of screwing up the economy.

AVOIDANCE | REVENGE STRATEGIES
1. Make yourself feel better by reading books on how the kings of England were killed when they became out of touch. Fantasise about how you would dispatch the Out of Touch Politician if you had the chance.

2. Buy into everything they say, as this is far better for your blood pressure and you certainly don't want to be going into hospital only to pick up MRSA.

3. Publish a book which translates politician speak into the language of the real world. This could include such things as: 'I can see the green shoots of recovery' = 'unemployment may be up, but have you seen China's?'; and 'British jobs for British workers' = 'Christ, I had better make sure I do something soon or else the funding from the Unions will go to the Tory party', etc.

4. Write a long and tortuous letter seeking clarification on the current economic difficulties and send it to the Chancellor. Use the response to judge just how out of touch he is.

5. Have millions of politician-dolls manufactured in China with the face imprinted on their bottoms (you could call them the 'Bullshit Doll'). Include a button to press which broadcasts the typical out of touch statements used by politicians. You should aim to get these into the toy shops in time for the Christmas rush.

THE OUT OF TOUCH POLITICIAN:

☐ Can blame someone else for their predicament

☐ Only has them self to blame

☐ Deserves our sympathy and should be hugged

☐ Deserves our contempt and should be shot

The Outbound Immigrant

The history of the human race has been marked by major migrations in population. Whether this was the result of war, famine, persecution or just the desire to scrounge off an overly generous state benefits system, migration has helped the global economy at the micro and macro levels for millennia. According to the United Nations, the number of people living outside their country of birth has nearly doubled over the last 50 years to a record 191 million. Interestingly, women make up almost half of the migrant population and those aged between 10 and 24, a third; one out of every four immigrants lives in the US and one in three in Europe. And thanks to things like globalisation, the ageing of the population and the creation of the European Union, economic migration has become all the rage for anyone who fancied getting a better job than they could at home. What set the UK aside as the destination of choice for immigrants both legal and illegal, however, was the generosity of the state benefits system. By merely entering UK airspace immigrants could have homes, cash, and copious amounts of support lavished on them by government officials who had long since given up on their usual clients – the indigenous workshy, long-term sick and NEETs (Not currently engaged in Employment, Education or Training). And as word got around that the UK taxpayer would be more than happy to pay for immigrants to hang around street corners, the trickle soon turned into a flood. Immigrants swarmed to the UK using every possible mode of transport – land, sea, air, the Channel Tunnel and the inside of unsuspecting holidaymakers' suitcases.

Before the Credit Crunch and the Great Recession, no one gave a stuff about immigration as at the time it made perfect sense to everyone. For the new generation of workshy lazy graduates and school leavers who felt the world owed them a living it meant they didn't have to do all the crap jobs which barely paid the minimum wage. For employers it meant they could pay the newly arrived immigrants virtually nothing, substantially increase their profit margins in the process and still get more work out of them in one day than they would out of their UK counterparts in a year. For consumers everywhere, it meant a return to the excellent service levels they had experienced just after the war when people smiled at you when they served you rather than shooting you dirty looks. For the black market employers it gave them a ready source of illegal labour which they could exploit and get rich off the back of. And lastly, let us not forget the immigrants themselves who although paid virtually nothing by our standards, were rich beyond their wildest dreams. After no time at all, immigrant workers were filling every single service job going and you would see them wherever you went. Meanwhile, all the lazy good for nothing British scroungers carried on claiming the benefits which where rightly theirs.

Now that things are just a little bit different the flood of immigrants is turning into a flood of Outbound Immigrants. All of a sudden people are getting mighty fed up that they are here and believe they have more than outstayed their welcome. Government

officials and benefits scroungers collectively agree that the UK has enough spongers already without the immigrant contingent adding to them. Workers too are up in arms because all of a sudden immigrants are taking jobs they actually want (I thought no one wanted to clean toilets and scrub floors these days?). Workers are going on strike because immigrant workers who are five thousand times more productive and infinitely better qualified are getting paid less than they are. Of course, it has nothing to do with what they are being paid and everything to do with highlighting just how unproductive and lazy British workers are. Fortunately Gordon Brown, in his infinite wisdom spouted the now infamous words 'British Jobs for British Workers' which was a sod-off charter for any immigrant who had a brain. Unfortunately for Gordon and of course the UK, all the wrong immigrants are now leaving – the smart, well educated and highly skilled ones – leaving us with the international terrorists (who always seem to be granted political asylum) and the benefits scroungers who are still very well looked after by government officials desperate not to be seen as racist, biased or politically incorrect. And as they disappear there is no one left to man our public toilets, serve us our food in restaurants, sweep the streets and do all the jobs that has kept the country going for the past decade or so. And do you really think that the newly qualified graduates and school leavers are going to pick up a bog brush and work for a living ... I don't think so.

The Outbound Immigrants are leaving the sinking ship, using every possible mode of transport – land, sea, air, the Channel Tunnel, and this time they are carrying the suitcases themselves.

☐ **Tick here when you have spotted the Outbound Immigrant**

SYMPATHY RATING – **8**
In some respects it is a shame that the immigrants are leaving as they added a bit of multicultural colour to an otherwise xenophobic nation. It is unfortunate but whenever there is a downturn everyone assumes that it is the immigrants' fault, even though we all know exactly who is to blame. Still, on the bright side, I am sure they will come back and visit us again one day, only next time as tourists.

RARITY – **6**
The Outbound Immigrants are steadily increasing and as the economy continues to shrink and the Pound gradually falls, their numbers will increase still further. And we all know that when the Euro is worth more than the Pound, it won't be just the immigrants who will be leaving.

WHAT ARE THEY DOING NOW?
Wishing they had settled in Japan, who are paying immigrants very handsomely to leave their country so long as they never come back. With the

average age of the Japanese citizen hovering around 102, it is highly unlikely that there will be anything left to come back to apart from a few robots clearing up all the rotting corpses – you can't fault Japanese innovation.

AVOIDANCE | REVENGE STRATEGIES

1. Don't assume that every immigrant is a scrounger, there to steal your job or claim state benefits which really belong to you. The majority are hard working and would never have the gall to claim for the stuff you do.

2. If you are looking for work there should be thousands of opportunities in the service economy now that the immigrants are leaving. You should literally be able to walk straight into a new role (yes even if you have no qualifications and can barely spell your name).

3. Shake the Outbound Immigrants by their hands and thank them for all their hard work over the years. As they turn to board the train, ferry or get into their Lada, carefully stick one of the 'British Jobs for British Workers' stickers on their back.

4. Buy an old luxury cruise liner and set up an Inbound-Outbound Immigration service. Pick up immigrants from those countries getting rid of their guest workers and take them to those countries still interested in having them. Charge a small fee for their upkeep whilst on board and offer them such things as lectures on the benefit systems of the countries they are going to and a few board games to keep them occupied on the long voyage.

5. Suggest to the Home Secretary that we create Fortress Britain and model ourselves on America. Suggest surrounding the British Isles with a 50 foot high steel barrier to prevent anyone who shouldn't be here from getting in. The beauty of this idea is that it will create many thousands of jobs for the low-skilled and newly unemployed (but not any immigrants of course).

THE OUTBOUND IMMIGRANT:

☐ Can blame someone else for their predicament

☐ Only has them self to blame

☐ Deserves our sympathy and should be hugged

☐ Deserves our contempt and should be shot

The Petty Thief

It is a well-known fact that when economies boom most people do well and even though some clearly do better than others, the majority of people are sufficiently content with their lot to be well behaved. As you'd expect crime tends to fall as people are far more interested in buying the latest Play Station 3 game than breaking into next door to steal it. So up until the Credit Crunch hit and everyone started losing their jobs, houses, spouses, pets and their self-esteem, thieves were mainly restricted to errant clowns who had nipped out between the matinee and evening shows of the visiting circus and members of the occasional traveller community who had just parked in the field up the road. Also, studies showed that during boom times people were more likely to wear pastel colours and skip to work. This gave the police force a much needed rest and gave them ample time to get to know the local community and to spend their time chasing pointless government targets relating to the fear of being hijacked whist on a tricycle.

Unfortunately now that the recession is in full flow crime figures are beginning to soar once more as people slide back down the income scale and get a tad more desperate. With a lower income, it becomes very difficult to maintain the lifestyle you had got used to and affording that new Play Station 3 game becomes that much harder (mind you at nearly £40, I think we all know who the bloody criminals are!). This means that the police have to start dealing with crime rather than the causes of crime. Known euphemistically as the 'Crunch Crime Wave' mainly because statisticians need to give names to things and alarmist daytime television presenters like to tell stories of park benches being stolen in broad daylight by gangs, we are in the middle of a veritable crime wave and it has to be said no one is safe. As people around the country break into their next door neighbours' shed and shimmy through their bathroom windows wearing a cat suit (or leotard and swimming goggles if they haven't managed to get hold of one), they are overwhelming the police force who are often otherwise occupied quelling the latest economic protest. Those who don't go in for the cat burgling approach to getting by are resorting to stealing pencils and staplers from their employers or using the photocopier more than they should. Such white collar crime is all the rage and you can see men and women in tweed suits being chased down the street by overweight and generally ineffective security guards, pockets bulging with Post-it notes and photocopier toner cartridges.

It doesn't take long for petty thievery to get out of hand though, especially in the United States where the gun laws are somewhat lax. Desperate times clearly call for desperate measures and tales of formerly fine upstanding deacons from local churches, soccer coaches for the under twos and volunteers who help build orphanages donning George Bush masks before robbing banks are increasingly common. Unlike professional felons, the hapless amateurs usually get caught and end up in jail. All cite deep financial woes caused by a combination of factors: the loss of a job, out of control credit card debt

and an obsession with Dolly Parton memorabilia. And although judges tend to look benevolently on the poor souls who are brought before them, it is usually the Dolly Parton thing that ends up taking them down for life.

Thankfully the government recognises the threat and is working with major retailers to offer significant discounts on security equipment; the 15% off is going to make massive inroads into reducing Credit Crunch Crime (or C³ as it is now known). In addition they are looking at paying local handymen to fit window locks and other security devices, which is an excellent plan, and one that many petty thieves will want to muscle in on (enquiring as to the owner's holiday plans while they're at it).

Fortunately, these difficult times are also making it much more tempting to shop your criminal friends to the police. Indeed, many are being shopped to the law in order to make ends meet. Tales of disgruntled drug addicts turning in their dealers because the cocaine wasn't pure enough, and wives suspicious that their criminal husband is having an affair with the local slapper are coming in thick and fast. And even the criminals themselves are getting in on the game by asking their friends to stitch them up so that they can share the reward (naturally after any stolen goods have either been fenced or hidden where they will never be found). As if to show just how desperate people have become, one guy even claimed to have seen Bin Laden in the frozen food aisle of his local Tesco; needless to say he wasn't successful in his claim as it turned out to be someone who had just returned from Guantanamo Bay.

 Tick here when you have spotted the Petty Thief

 SYMPATHY RATING – **3**
Although breaking the law is of course wrong and no one likes to have their house broken into or indeed their personal possessions stolen, we are in difficult times and people are getting desperate. As money runs out and as state handouts become stingier people have no choice but to find other ways to make ends meet.

 RARITY – **3**
Although there has been an increase in petty crime since the recession kicked in, this has yet to get completely out of hand. However as it drags on and as banks refuse to lend money hand over fist like they used to, the numbers of Petty Thieves will balloon. Only once we pull out of recession can we return to the good old days of wearing pastel clothes and pinching pencils from the office to help the kids along with their homework.

 WHAT ARE THEY DOING NOW?
Donning a pair of their wife's black denier tights, a skin tight spandex all in one outfit (used by theatrical types who move props around) and

creeping out the back door in the dead of night. Soon to be seen tiptoeing through the local allotments procuring (on a permanent basis) assorted fruit, vegetables and garden implements. If not stealing from allotments, they will be climbing into the bedrooms of sleeping children and pinching the latest Play Station 3 game.

AVOIDANCE | REVENGE STRATEGIES
1. Avoid having your house burgled by purchasing sturdy metal security doors and windows which will make the house completely airtight. Also consider putting razor wire and broken glass along all your window sills like Charles Bronson did in 'Vigilante II'.

2. Campaign to bring back 'Police Five', that wonderful 1970s Sunday afternoon television programme with Shaw Taylor, and use each five minute slot to bring peoples' attention to the latest petty crime perpetrated by some pensioner desperate for a hot meal. Remember to throw in the catch phrase – 'Keep 'em peeled'.

3. Set up a local C³ crime unit modelled on the Bow Street Runners and track down the petty thieves. Once you have cornered them in a side alley break their kneecaps with your heavy wooden truncheon.

4. Have the Crime stoppers telephone redirected to you so that you get to hear about all the crimes before the police do. Take a note of their names, addresses and heinous acts, shop them to the local police and claim the reward. The way the crime wave is panning out, you will soon be rich beyond your wildest dreams.

5. Why not join in the current crime wave yourself by offering to fence stolen goods? There are plenty of car boot sales where you could pass the property off and you could take a 10% cut. Watch out for those vultures, though, (you know, the people who swarm all over you as soon as you open the boot of your car). They never want to give you a decent price – bloody crooks.

THE PETTY THIEF:

☐ Can blame someone else for their predicament

☐ Only has them self to blame

☐ Deserves our sympathy and should be hugged

☐ Deserves our contempt and should be shot

The Pissed-off State Pensioner

When the whole concept of pension provision was first suggested by Otto von Bismarck in 1881 and subsequently adopted in 1889, it seemed like a perfect idea ... at the time. It was designed to provide a social welfare safety net for the older folk in work so that they could continue to be as productive as possible for as long as possible, and when they were truly worn out and of no use to anyone anymore, the state would pay them a bit of cash until they died. Trust the Germans to be ruthlessly efficient by making everyone work like dogs, but that's what made them great and of course capable of occupying France on multiple occasions; the French, on the other hand, were workshy and too busy drinking red wine and coffee to be bothered which of course explains at lot. The other interesting thing about Bismarck's idea was that the age at which such benefits were to be paid was set at 70, when it was highly likely that anyone who lived that long would be as much use as a chocolate teacup. Given that the life expectancy of the average German at that time was well below 40, the likelihood of the benefits ever having to be paid out was very remote indeed, (although I believe Bismarck managed to squeeze a few deutschmarks out of the system as he lived to 74). Bismarck was a very clever man – he gave the illusion that he cared knowing he would never have to come good on his promise, and died well before the shit hit the fan. The perfect politician if ever there was one. It didn't take long for the whole world to latch onto the idea of pensions for the elderly, and before you could say World War One, every country worth its salt was setting up similar schemes.

It was only after Bismarck died that everything started to unravel. First the Germans decided to reduce the age at which the pensions would be paid to 65, which obviously seemed like a good idea at the time. But then we all started to benefit from the increased longevity that came with improved healthcare, diet and housing and soon the numbers reaching 65 increased, causing all sorts of havoc. In the UK alone we now have something in the region of 12 million pensioners, and this increases every second of every day. The same of course is true in every developed nation around the world apart from Russia where they still drink themselves to death by the time they reach 40.

Being the tight-fisted, means–testing obsessed nation that we are, pensioners in the UK only get a few pence to live off and this explains why they are such a dour lot. Mind you back in 1908 when pensions were introduced they were not so much means-tested, as character-tested. So, if you were a workshy ex-con who was always drunk you got nothing (and quite rightly too).

Today's state pensioners are very, very, pissed-off and this has got progressively worse as the Credit Crunch has crunched on. The things they have to put up with include:

- Having the crappiest state pension in Europe, if not the world. Compared to our counterparts in Europe, our state pensions are derisory.
- Receiving no interest on their savings and in many cases having to pay banks to hold onto their cash.
- Being conned out of their money by evil financial advisors who recommend that they invest what little cash they have in interest rate swaps, structured products or junk bonds. The advisor gets a tidy commission and the pensioner gets a seizure.
- Having to wait until they are 80 to receive an extra 40 pence a week top-up to allow them to pay for a bag of coal.
- Having to queue up at tea dances to be given a manky plain digestive and some lukewarm tea.
- Fighting over second-hand jumpers and tights at jumble sales, which these days resemble the first day of the Harrods Sale.

You can always tell the state pensioner from the many lucky pensioners who benefited from decent company schemes by their pallid skin, toothless smile and the two-bar electric fire they can only afford to run one bar of. Things are undoubtedly bad and many pensioners have cut back on heating, food, seeing friends and even attending funerals. Others are resorting to the reckless behaviour of their children by draining what little equity they have in their homes. You can't blame them because their kids refuse to look after them, so they might as well spend the whole damn lot and go massively into debt just before they die; that'll teach 'em!

☐ **Tick here when you have spotted the Pissed-off State Pensioner**

SYMPATHY RATING – 9
I think it is tough for pensioners trying to get by on a fixed income which drops in real terms each year (well until we have a period of deflation of course, in which case they will be quids in). As all of us will eventually become one, showing a bit of sympathy is important. Of course, try telling that to the poor bastards who are going to have to pay for them all and I am sure the sympathy drops right off. Let's face it, with too few young people in work (or wanting to work); all the clever people fleeing the country and immigrants leaving with their tails between their legs, there won't be anyone left to pay for anything, let alone the pension of someone they don't even know.

RARITY – 8
Given the parlous state of the nation's finances right now, I cannot see the pensioner community returning to their cheery outlook anytime soon. Plus with more pensioners joining their ranks every day, we will soon be drowned out by all the complaining about the cost of living this, and of course, lazy good for nothing, hoody wearing young people. Thank heavens for the iPod.

WHAT ARE THEY DOING NOW?
If not covering themselves up with 30 woollen blankets in an attempt to keep warm, they will be joining many of the pensioner-rights protests and smashing the windows of those greedy corporate bankers – after all, it's all their fault.

AVOIDANCE | REVENGE STRATEGIES
1. Try and support pensioners as much as you can; most of them fought for you on the beaches of Normandy and deserve a decent retirement. Ask yourself what you can do for them, not what they can knit for you.

2. If you happen to have the odd pensioner or two knocking about your cupboards at home, pack them off to an old people's home as quickly as possible. Before you do so, sign all their money into a trust so that you don't pay a dime to the taxman or indeed the home, (it's about time the state paid up on something). Once they are out of the way, lavish the cash on lots of overseas holidays. Hell, take them with you – the beauty of having someone old and infirm travelling with you is that you stand more chance of being upgraded to First Class.

3. Go and live in Greece, as their pensions are fantastic. Plus you can enjoy the Mediterranean lifestyle that all the doctors and health gurus freak out about. Which means you can sit around in the sun drinking ouzo and eating olives until well into your 90s. It certainly beats Glasgow's East End where they drink whisky and eat deep fried Mars Bars until well into their early 50s.

4. Develop a pensioner's money-saving website which promotes the plight of the millions of pensioners living below the breadline. If you are lucky you will invited to speak in the House of Commons and appear on daytime TV. After a while you may become a minor celebrity and be able to star in various reality TV shows such as 'I'm a Celebrity, Get me out of Here' where you can lecture the other contestants about pensioners. I would be careful though, as this is likely to get you voted off in the first week.

5. Recommend to the government that in order to solve the aging population problem they should revisit Bismarck's principles and raise the pensionable age to 95. In that way only a small percentage of people will be able to claim a pension and it will save billions. It will also eliminate the need to tax everyone to death; just work them to death instead.

THE PISSED-OFF STATE PENSIONER:

☐ Can blame someone else for their predicament

☐ Only has them self to blame

☐ Deserves our sympathy and should be hugged

☐ Deserves our contempt and should be shot

The Ponzi Schemer

Back in the summer of 1920, when the Great War was rapidly becoming a distant memory and the Wall Street Crash was still a long way off, an Italian immigrant by the name of Charles Ponzi happened to come up with a cunning scheme to fleece unsuspecting, naive and incredibly stupid investors. Ponzi's idea was very simple and highly effective. He promised to double an investor's money in three months. At a time when the average annual salary was $2000 and the price of a can of codfish cakes was a mere 25 cents (clearly something that the people of Boston chose to eat instead of something that was force fed to the inmates of the state penitentiary), Ponzi's scheme was a no brainer. So along they came in their thousands, mugs from all walks of life driven by greed and an insatiable appetite for more codfish cakes; investing like crazy in a scheme that would make them insanely rich without ever lifting a finger. Well apart from one thing of course – it wouldn't. Ponzi's shrewd plan was to pay the promised returns of the early investors with the deposits of the later ones. There was no magic formula, no intelligent investment strategy, merely a process of robbing Peter to pay Paul, or robbing Mary to pay Maud (for the politically correct amongst the readership). At its height, Ponzi's scheme was pulling in $2 million a week and when it all came tumbling down a few months later people lost pretty much everything. As for Ponzi, after a spell inside the state penitentiary, most likely spent picking-up soap from the shower room floor, he was deported and eventually died in a charity ward of a Rio de Janeiro hospital in 1948. At the time of his death, he had £75 to his name, not even enough for a decent burial. Hopefully a nurse quietly pocketed the cash and got smashed on tequila and then threw Ponzi's body into the street to be picked apart by vultures and the local inhabitants of a nearby shanty town.

Ponzi may be dead, but his name lives on and as the Credit Crunch and recession continue to take their toll, more and more equally smarmy miscreants continue to fleece the unsuspectingly naive or incredibly stupid investor. Clearly, some things never change. Take Bernie Madoff, that grease ball New Yorker who looks as though he has been smacked with a wet fish, clearly wanting to outdo the erstwhile Ponzi, screwed his clients for a cool $64 billion. Like Ponzi, he was a smooth-talking, rich-living charmer who was able to grease his way into the wallets of the great and the good. As he sauntered around the exclusive resorts and golf courses of the world he claimed to be able to offer returns of 46% a year whilst in reality he didn't invest a dime of his client's money. Yes, even those who are meant to be smarter than us can be suckers for the 'get rich quick', 'no risk/high return' models of investing too; they assume that a 46% return on their money year after year is quite normal, (which suggests they have the financial literacy of a frog). As the list of celebrities duped by Madoff grew longer, they all claimed that they thought Bernie was a genuine guy who was capable of pulling-of a miraculous investment strategy equivalent to turning water into wine. Perhaps it was his big cow eyes, or his lovely tan that convinced them.

As this geezer is in his seventies and possibly not long for this world, he decided to tell his adoring (and of course exceedingly well paid) sons that he was a crook. As fine upstanding citizens they duly turned their old man into the Feds. However, even as the net closed in, he was busy writing cheques for millions of dollars to his wife and stuffing envelopes full of diamonds to send to his relations to make sure that no one would get their hands on his well-earned cash,. When he appeared in court he expressed how grateful he was to be given the chance to let everyone know how sorry and ashamed he was and to own up to knowing that he was breaking the law all along and would eventually be found out (like that was a revelation to anyone). Still, having enjoyed life to the full on other people's money I guess he can look back with few regrets. Given that he has now been sentenced to 150 years in jail, I am sure his cheesy, supercilious look and beautiful tan will soon be replaced by the haggard look of a condemned man – no Club Fed for him. Perhaps the medical profession should keep him alive using stem cells so that he actually serves the entire term – and has to learn to enjoy picking up soap in the prison showers with a big grin on his face.

☐ **Tick here when you have spotted the Ponzi Schemer (and make it particularly large if you have been fleeced by one)**

SYMPATHY RATING – 1
Although I have not been personally impacted by the Ponzi Schemer, I can see why people could be a tad annoyed and generally unsympathetic to the poor Ponzi Schemer's plight. Having placed your trust in a smooth talking, larger than life 'cheeky chap', who subsequently spends all your money living big with his friends and family, pretending to be a pillar of society, you would feel kind of cheated and indeed very, very, stupid. If it was me, I would keep quiet.

RARITY – 6
As the Credit Crunch continues to weave its way across the world, other Ponzi schemes continue to emerge. Madoff has already been joined by a clutch of mid-ranking Ponzis (after all I can't see him being beat anytime soon), each with their own unique qualities. One recent example involved a pair of hedge fund managers who lived large on the $553 million they misappropriated from their investors. One of them loved teddy bears so much that he spent $80000 on them. Maybe his mother didn't love him enough as a child, or perhaps he had no real friends. Whatever the reason, I am sure he will ask the judge if he can take them with him as he is sent down. He could always use them to fill out his mattress or provide him with some special comfort during those long dark and lonely nights..

WHAT ARE THEY DOING NOW?
If they are not currently on the run, you will find them spending their remaining days on this earth in an eight foot by eight foot prison cell,

crapping into a toilet without a seat, using their hand to wipe their bottom and sharing their accommodation with a couple of burly Columbian drug dealers with too much time on their hands (and who are no doubt teaching the Ponzi Schemer to touch his toes).

AVOIDANCE | REVENGE STRATEGIES
1. If you really want to avoid the Ponzi Schemer, live by the simple maxim – if it's too good to be true, then it probably is.

2. If you want to keep your money safe, invest it in gold or perhaps even a failed bank, after all, you probably own it.

3. Ask for your money back from any dodgy sounding investment, you know things like hedge funds, exchange traded options, pension funds and the like.

4. Take matters into you own hands and organise a lynch mob. Track the Ponzi Schemer down and hang them from the nearest lamppost. Once you're done take a couple of pictures and upload them to MySpace or You Tube.

5. Write to your MP and ask that they bring back Tyburn public executions – it will certainly draw a crowd and if you are really smart, why not charge an entrance fee?

THE PONZI SCHEMER:

☐ Can blame someone else for their predicament

☐ Only has them self to blame

☐ Deserves our sympathy and should be hugged

☐ Deserves our contempt and should be shot

The Pseudo Rich

Anyone with half a brain understands that most celebrities are air-headed narcissists who add as much value to society as an elected official, and if only to prove the point some actually end up elected, which makes them doubly useless. I would go further and say that most of them are full of crap. They would be nothing of course without their adoring single-celled fans, it's just unfortunate that there is such a significant number of said amoeba-brained citizens out there. These celeb-obsessed cretins like nothing better than to feast on the latest round of celebrity gossip. From stars with hearts who purchase their children from any continent with a low GDP, to soap actors and footballers being arrested for drink driving (again). Indeed, for many a youth these days the only thing they aspire to is to 'be famous', to become a celebrity in their own right and Paris Hilton's new best friend. Why exactly? Who are these empty headed prepubescent girls who can barely muster a GCSE in media studies or these overly-effeminate boys who wear flip-flops and carry man-bags? With real fame and fortune out of reach, the only thing left for the hapless celebrity lover is to emulate the celeb lifestyle, and with so much freely-available credit they were able to do just that, despite the fact that unlike their heroes who have bottomless wells of cash, the wannabes only have a Barclaycard with a £2500 limit.

The Pseudo Rich, as I like to call these sad individuals, like to spend well beyond their means, maxing out on every possible credit line they can secure. They will buy whatever their favourite celeb happens to be wearing, be that a wildly expensive haute couture ball gown, overpriced sunglasses, or, God forbid, one of those ridiculously priced Louis Vuitton handbags that looks as though a retard has written all over it. Even metrosexuals use them which just shows how bad things have got; it was celebrities like David Beckham that ushered in such a phenomenon. The traditional male had finally become completely emasculated (by female zealots wanting to crush the male gender of course), replaced by the modern 'metrosexual', typified by their use of perfume, moisturiser, flip-flops, three-quarter length flared trousers and colourful sarongs. For those blokes who clearly latched onto the whole metrosexual movement, it was a no brainer – off they rushed to chemists and designer outlets to emulate their metrosexual heroes. I wonder if they gave up reading and writing too.

The Pseudo Rich believe quite wrongly of course, that if they walk around in expensive clothes, fancy shoes and celebrity endorsed make-up and perfume it will somehow all conspire to make them appear wealthy and important. Not only that, they also believe that those around them will do a double take thinking they have just had someone fabulously wealthy and famous breeze past them. It is clear, however, to all normal people that that they look more like mutton dressed as lamb, and when they open their mouths and enunciate in their estuary English or incomprehensible regional dialogue, it is even more comprehensively clear that they could never be someone famous, just famously in debt.

Pull back the veneer of pseudo richness and you will see that the person behind it is nothing more than Mr, Mrs or Miss Below Average. Such people have never amounted to much and arguably never will, principally because they lack any true ability. They hold down low end service jobs, live with their parents or in rented accommodation and spend more than they earn on attempting to look rich. But since the Credit Crunch the Pseudo Rich have fast become the Real Poor as their credit lines have dried up and the expensive clothes and lotions have become well and truly out of their reach. Like so many who believed that paying for everything on credit was in effect free money they have woken up to a Credit Crunch nightmare. Pass the tissues.

☐ **Tick here when you have spotted the Pseudo Rich**

SYMPATHY RATING – 1
Why people just can't be themselves and accept who they are and their lot in life, I just don't know. The level of sympathy for the Pseudo Rich has to be low for a variety of good reasons, not least for their gullibility, obsession with celebrities and over spending habits. Sure, if you want to worship celebs restrict your spending to publications such as 'Hello!' or 'OK' magazine; they are much cheaper and you can still get your fix of mind numbing trash. Wasting unnecessary amounts of money on celebrity endorsed products which are still manufactured in the sweatshops of Asia is only something that cretins do. It's time to grow up.

RARITY – 7
There is a direct correlation between the rise in celebrity culture and the Pseudo Rich. What is especially interesting about this correlation is that it looks remarkably like the famous 'hockey stick' shaped graph associated with the impact of global warming and I am beginning to wonder if the two are related?

WHAT ARE THEY DOING NOW?
Wearing clothes from Primark, hiding from their creditors and refusing to open any envelope that looks remotely like a credit card bill. They are also economising on the celebrities they want to emulate, 'trading down' to some of the 'D' listed celebs who are promoting cheap clothing from high street chain stores and food from Iceland. Of course, one has to remember that the said celebs wouldn't be seen dead in such featureless clothing or eating such over-processed dog food, and as soon the photo shoot of them looking happy to be wearing a paper thin trouser suit scoffing frozen vol-au-vents is over, and they change back into their haute couture slacks and stop by The Ivy for dinner.

AVOIDANCE | REVENGE STRATEGIES
1. Steer clear of any celebrity and certainly don't emulate them; you just look stupid and it will only get you into debt. What's more it doesn't make you look wealthy – just someone common wanting to be wealthy.

2. Lecture them on the error of their ways by pointing out to them that most of the things that celebrities wear are patently too expensive and well beyond the reach of a shop assistant with three GCSEs.

3. Make a placard which says 'The end of the Pseudo Rich is nigh' and walk around large out of town shopping centres. Ideally you should wear as much celebrity endorsed clothing and perfume as possible.

4. Pose as a celebrity makeover expert, offering your services to the Pseudo Rich. Charge them a lot of money to recommend face lifts and ensure they have the right wardrobe to match their favoured star, (Victoria Beckham's little black dress, Gok Wan's glasses – even if they're not short-sighted – and Simon Cowell's trousers).

5. Launch a celebrity credit card which offers those who want to be like their favourite celebrity the ability to print a picture of the celeb on the card. Offer money off vouchers for celebrity endorsed goods, and don't forget to charge an extortionate APR, something like 85.67% should do the trick.

THE PSEUDO RICH:

☐ Can blame someone else for their predicament

☐ Only has them self to blame

☐ Deserves our sympathy and should be hugged

☐ Deserves our contempt and should be shot

The Relegated Rich

There is always this view that once you become wealthy you don't need to worry about anything else ever again. You have the money to do what you want, you can treat everyone in the service industry with contempt and you might even be able to cheat death. Oh, if only that were true. You see the wealthy (hedge fund managers, CEOs of major businesses, footballers, film stars, pop stars, soap stars and the odd oligarch or two) are really no better than the middle classes with all their petty boasting and one-upmanship, they just have a bit more cash to do it with. You can find them at parties (glamorised in 'Hello!' and similar rags aimed at those unable to read), in San Tropez, or at the Oscars showing other wealthy people photos of their latest 5000 foot yacht or the island they have just bought in a hitherto unchartered part of the South Pacific. Not to be outdone, others will show off their 5005 foot yacht just to prove they are better than the jerk with his 5000 foot vessel who will then leave the event depressed and unable to satisfy his beautiful girlfriend hanging onto his carefully waxed arm. Then there are the parties in which naked images of the host and hostess are carved out of a piece of collapsed Arctic ice shelf which has been shipped in and sculpted especially for the occasion. And the grandiose charity events where they will make huge financial gestures to help the endangered tap dancers of Outer Mongolia. It's a classic case of 'status anxiety' with the volume turned up to full.

What has made this ten times worse is the ranking and yanking of the wealthy in these tacky rich lists that come out every year. They're a bit like the performance tables published for schools that show 'The Warbler School for the Great Unwashed' managed to achieve an average of ½ a GCSE in grades A* to C, itself an improvement over last year which brings them up from 4590 to 3600 on the UK's 4600 'schools to die for' list. So I wonder how the Queen feels having been knocked off the rich list by a banker, politician or worst of all, a celebrity? Probably okay because she is after all, the Queen and no one can beat that, not even Elton John. As the years have gone by such lists have become more stupid by including information about things like the best star signs of the rich (for those interested, Taurus is the new Gemini apparently; so that's me screwed then), or who the richest person with sciatica is this year.

With Schadenfreude all the rage, it is actually quite funny to see that the rich are also seeing their net worth dropping like a stone. And apart from those silly enough to be fleeced by the likes of Bernie Madoff and the other Ponzi Schemers, the Relegated Rich have seen their wealth tank as their properties, investments and shoe collections have fallen off a cliff. It must be terribly hard for a once self important billionaire to hold his or her head up in public now that they have to mix with mere millionaires, (I mean how disgusting). So, given that the number of billionaires has fallen from 1125 to a paltry 793 there must be plenty of crushed egos out there who feel ashamed to call themselves rich. The class war fans amongst the readership will be glad to know that the 1000 richest people in the UK have collectively lost £155 billion in wealth, and the

Russians (who got rich by buying [stealing] all the Soviet assets for a couple of Roubles following the collapse of the communist empire) have had their money taken back by the state and have been thrown into jail; and let's not even mention the Icelanders (at least they can still shop at Iceland).

It seems that the biggest winners are the divorcees who saw that their spouses were going down the toilet and quite wisely bailed out of a loveless marriage at just the right time; they can now run off into the sunset with a Brazilian Adonis and although they may look like wizened crones, I am sure the toy boy will manage to fake sexual excitement, so long as everything is done in the pitch black.

The rich are like the rest of us in having to economise and although I don't see many of them in the aisles at Aldi just yet, many are deeply worried that they may end up running out of money and a lot feel less confident than they used to, (mainly because they have had to let their body guards go). Many are cutting back – 80% are looking to save money, 77% were buying fewer big ticket items (I am assuming here white goods and flat screen televisions – diamond studded of course) and 78% were waiting for the sales. But the one area where they really ought to be cutting back on is spending on their pretentious brats. One little darling had 300 guests to her 16th birthday party along with a bunch of tigers, elephants and even a Ferris wheel. Another had the invitations delivered by models, but it was a case of no present, no party. One can only hope that when their parents go bust they will have to make do with a happy meal at MacDonald's and a clown who makes obscene models out of colourful balloons.

☐ **Tick here when you have spotted the Relegated Rich**

SYMPATHY RATING – 1
As someone who is not in any way wealthy and is unlikely to be anytime soon, I can't shed many tears when I hear that the super rich have lost a few bob here and there. In the great scheme of things they may have dropped a few hundred million, but compared to the average salary of a tree surgeon, it still looks like a shed load of cash. Of course, if I happened to be very rich then I would be making a big song and dance about it all, crying in front of the television cameras and seeking some bailout cash from the government.

RARITY – 1
With the world's population hovering around 6.77 billion, the number of millionaires and billionaires is nothing more than a wormhole on a freshly ploughed lawn. And let's face it, do you really think that the billions on less than $1 a day could give a flying fork? I doubt it.

WHAT ARE THEY DOING NOW?
Poring over their investments and seeing how much of their losses are tax deductible. Unfortunately they soon realise that they can't offset anything

against tax, because they have been evading it for so long that if they did so, they would be spending a few years in a cell next to Bernie Madoff. If not worrying about their investments, you will find them scouring Tiffany's and other high end shops along Fifth Avenue and the Champs Elysee for cut price jewellery, handbags, shoes and designer clothes and then haggling with the shop assistant when they come to pay. Apparently the negotiation strategy often pays off, the rich it seems drive a hard bargain.

AVOIDANCE | REVENGE STRATEGIES
1. Don't worry about the rich, after all they don't worry about you. In any case it's good that they will be adopting a lower profile for a while.

2. Set yourself up as a thrift advisor to the rich. Offer your services to any rich person who has lost a substantial slice of their wealth. Include such things as yacht, wardrobe and diamond audits and make them list out their income and expenditure. Having completed this, lecture them on the importance of keeping to a budget and avoiding dodgy financial investments.

3. Organise a car boot sale for the rich and famous in the grounds of a stately home. Ensure that only top-end cars are given access, like Rolls Royces and Bentleys. Charge a £1500 entrance fee to sellers and a £2000 fee for buyers.

4. Pose as a tramp, but with a twist. Deck yourself out in all the latest designer clothing, including a nice handbag (or man bag, whichever is appropriate) and hang around Bond Street or Fifth Avenue with a hand written note on a piece of discarded cardboard 'Fallen on hard times – 15 homes, a castle and two mistresses to maintain ... £50 notes only please!'

5. Develop a real-time '100 most wealthy people' monitor and install it in Times Square, New York. Link it directly to the New York Stock Exchange and property prices and have the Mayor of New York ring a bell at the end of each day to signify who has made it to the top. Use a dustbin symbol for those who have fallen off the bottom and have a random celebrity stand next to the Mayor each day.

THE RELEGATED RICH:

☐ Can blame someone else for their predicament

☐ Only has them self to blame

☐ Deserves our sympathy and should be hugged

☐ Deserves our contempt and should be shot

The Repossessed

Many people around the world have been caught up in the crazy property bubble where buying and selling property became the new designer drug of choice. As prices continued to rise year on year and showed no sign of abating, everyone felt compelled to jump into the market and stake their claim on a beautiful Tuscan house on the edge of an amazing vineyard or a one bed maisonette overlooking the river Nidd. It didn't matter what the cost was or indeed that the house was a derelict shit hole, they had to have it as if they didn't they would be *left behind* and would never, ever be able to buy anything or look their friends and family in the eye again. They would become the worst possible thing in the modern world – someone who had no property to live in, rent out or boast about. So, just like the Tulip Bubble, the South Sea Bubble and the Dotcom Bubble they were sucked into the property bubble and thought it could never end. Taking no notice that prices seemed a bit frothy and in order to secure the loan, eye watering multiples of their income were required, they continued to buy, buy, buy. After all, interest rates were cheap and the repayments were only taking 75% of their take home pay, so there was a little bit left over to eat and pay the mobile phone bill. Who cared when they had the Nidd-side views and the house was going up in value by more than £20 000 a week? At the same time of course, property developers continued to throw up new builds to meet the insatiable demand for riverside apartments and flats next to, or on top of, busy railway lines.

Like most bubbles, economic or otherwise, of course it went pop and although the first pop could be heard in the US, it wasn't long before there were popping noises across the world. Once the popping noises had stopped they were replaced with what sounded like farting noises. Again, starting in the US, the breaking of the property market wind could be heard across the world as home owners and property investors collectively shat themselves. I am sure that global warming has little to do with factory emissions and everything to do with the all that methane that has been released simultaneously across the globe from homeowners' bottoms.

As house prices started to go into freefall and as homeowners and property investors began to struggle to repay their loans, the number of repossessions shot up, once again led from the front by the Americans who were being foreclosed on by the banks who in turn needed to get rid of all their toxic loans (and at rates not seen since the Civil War). The property bubble had well and truly gone into reverse as the repossessed houses that were dumped onto the market at rock bottom prices only served to depress prices even further. And with the repossessions came the Repossessed. Faced with the simple choice of eating leftovers or, God forbid, shopping at Iceland, the Repossessed did whatever any sensible person staring disaster in the face would do, they followed the 'Four Steps to Repossession':

• Step 1 – have a round table discussion with your family, which usually involves shouting, screaming and the throwing of cutlery and bone china followed by tears. It's always good to clear the air and determine exactly who's to blame.

- Step 2 – develop a cunning plan to dodge the repossession bullet which involves selling grandfather's Victoria Cross, holding a garage sale and growing your own food.
- Step 3 – run out of cash and options, and more critically, develop food poisoning from eating rancid leftovers and be rushed to Accident and Emergency.
- Step 4 – rent a van, pack up the house and leave the country.

As property went belly up the number of Repossessed (or Foreclosed as they are termed in the US) grew and grew and in many ways mirrored the property bubble that preceded it. Hundreds of thousands joined the ranks of the Repossessed and tales of woe from young couples who only wanted to have a roof over their head to over-stretched egotists who had to ditch their 15 bed country pile littered the press. Off they marched to the nearest Estate Agent to throw the front door key through the window and then it was off to the Housing Association to see if there were any recently vacated bedsits available within walking distance of the local chip shop.

Although the plight of the Repossessed is bad, it is made a whole lot worse by the vultures that typically come out when bubbles burst. Like the local peasants who would rifle though the butchered armies on windswept English moors in the 1460s to steal the odd ring from the finger of a fallen knight, the vultures pick over the repossessed properties to get a good deal. Aided and abetted by companies who buy up tranches of repossessed properties from banks desperate to offload them, the property vultures are whipped up into a frenzy by the tuxedo wearing knobs that run around the auction hall goading the would-be buyers to bid for the latest property up for grabs shouting 'Bid! Bid! Bid!' Like modern-day court jesters, and using whistles, tambourines and symbols to stir up the crowd, they skip around high-fiving the successful bidders and then do cartwheels across the floor to Michael Jackson's 'Thriller'.

☐ **Tick here when you have spotted the Repossessed**

SYMPATHY RATING – **6**
The level of sympathy that should be dished out to the Repossessed will naturally vary according to their circumstances. It is very sad to see someone who was desperate to get a toehold on the property ladder fall off again. The same it has to be said for families who have found themselves on Queer Street and as a result have had to throw in the towel. However, those who should have known better and were merely trading up because they thought that owning bigger and bigger properties was the path to riches, deserve everything they get.

RARITY – **5**
Although not yet at an all time high (in this country at least), the numbers of the Repossessed are increasing dramatically and will continue to increase until such time as house prices drop back down to a reasonable level so that people can actually afford them, which by all accounts might be sometime between

2013 and 2017. Until then, you will see them peering at the repossessed houses on offer at the local Estate Agents with all their worldly possessions in a wheeled case behind them.

WHAT ARE THEY DOING NOW?
Trying to force their worldly goods that used to fit quite comfortably in their McMansion into a council owned one bed house on the edge of some long since disused railway siding whilst trying to figure out how they will ever get back onto the property ladder again. Still, at least they can watch re-runs of their favourite property shows and reminisce about the times when they owned a £700 000 property whilst on the income of a part-time child entertainer.

AVOIDANCE | REVENGE STRATEGIES
1. Never buy a house; in the long run it's a waste of money and will only make you poor. It is far better to rent as you won't pay as much, you will never be repossessed and you don't have to fix the toilet when it leaks.

2. If you happen to be flush at the moment why not pick up one of the recently repossessed properties; there is no doubt that you can get a real bargain right now and you'd be a fool to miss out.

3. Launch a new property programme that's ripe for the recession. Call it 'Reverse Property Ladder' and instead of seeing how much money you can earn from the booming property market, see how much money you can lose.

4. Ask the government to bailout all property owners so that everyone can live in a council house. This will not only eliminate the obsession with property but will also wipe out all mortgage arrears overnight and of course no one will ever be repossessed again. It will also herald in the much talked about 'classless Britain'.

5. Set up your own property company that offloads one of the million or so properties that have been repossessed. To make it more exciting hold all your sales in a circus tent with trapeze artists and lion tamers. Every time one of the repossessed properties is sold fire the winning bidder out of a cannon.

THE REPOSSESSED:

☐ Can blame someone else for their predicament

☐ Only has them self to blame

☐ Deserves our sympathy and should be hugged

☐ Deserves our contempt and should be shot

The Savvy Squatter

The recession has taken a terrible toll on the housing market. For almost two decades prices have been steadily rising and the demand for more houses, flats, McMansions, condominiums, holiday apartments, seaside chalets and garden sheds has gone through the roof. And in response property developers as well as amateur chancers have been building on every piece of spare land they could find and every acre they could get the government to release, including nuclear waste sites, ponds and disused mines. Supply kept on increasing in expectation that the whole of the country would become amateur landlords (including children under 16, the infirm, prisoners and the unborn) and that the millions of immigrants flooding across the border would mop up any excess stock. It seemed like a damn good idea and an obvious way to make pots of cash. Then we had the Credit Crunch and with that came the realisation that most of the mortgages were subprime and many of the people who took them out were idiots (as were the banks that lent to them). Property prices crashed through the floor, people lost their homes and millions of houses, flats, condominiums, seaside chalets and garden sheds were left empty.

Although a shame for the people who have been caught up in the basket case known as the property sector, one group has done exceedingly well out of it and that's the squatters. Despite most people thinking that squatters are disgusting people who never wash and who poo on carpets, they in fact come from a long line of Prussian kings who fell on hard times back in the 1880s after falling out with Bismarck. That said, of course, there are plenty of copycat squatters who don't wash and have been known to defecate on shag pile carpets, especially when they are about to be evicted. However despite their lack of personal hygiene, they are clever people who have spotted a gap in the housing market. And rather than share a hostel with loads of homeless bums who steal what little possessions you have and urinate over you when you are asleep, the Savvy Squatter will locate to a nice suburban house that is lying empty, tell their mates and before you can say 'knife' are living as one big happy family. The very smart ones will take their time to look for multimillion pound houses which have been left empty by their former owners – most notably the bankers who are now squatters themselves and of course the Russian Oligarchs who have been tracked down by the Russian Secret Service and taken back to the Motherland to spend the rest of their lives down a salt mine. Spending time in a multimillion pound house on the outskirts of London is a squatter's dream, and knowing all the tricks of the trade, they will do their utmost to stay there as long as possible.

Fortunately for the Savvy Squatter they often have plenty of help at hand from the Advisory Service for Squatters who for a couple of quid will give them plenty of tips including how to remove locks, how to obtain free legal advice and what kinds of notices to put on the door to deter would be burglars, government officials and the owners of the property from kicking them out. They also encourage as many people as

possible to become squatters by suggesting that only a small minority ever get arrested. Although most people think this kind of support is wrong, many councils direct would-be squatters to the Advisory Service, so it can't be all that bad. And if the Savvy Squatter is exceptionally savvy and spends many years in the same empty property it will eventually be theirs to own. In fact, if they hang on until the next property boom they might make a mint.

Although our Savvy Squatters like to think they are pretty cool, they are amateurs compared to their American counterpart who are no doubt the best squatters in the world and deserve the title 'Super Savvy Squatters'. Unlike ours, who just break into an empty property and wait until they get evicted by the police, the Americans take a different tack; they prepare counterfeit deeds (freely available online apparently), take possession of the property and then let their fellow squatters spend some time there. So instead of making do without electricity, gas and water like our squatters have to, our American brethren are able to live like kings with all the amenities available to them until they are evicted or paid to bugger off. One such guy calls himself King Solomon II and is busy misappropriating foreclosed property throughout Riverside County using deeds which have been signed and lodged with the county recorder. Claiming to be a religious organisation and therefore above any law it seems that King Solomon II is following in the footsteps of his more famous ancestor, (although for the record the original King Solomon did not misappropriate that much). Allegedly, once he has secured a property he displays a 'notice of forfeit' in the window that claims the legal owner has 24 days, excluding the Sabbath, to accept an amount of silver as payment for the property. And if you are wondering what the hell that means, then you'd better read the Bible and more specifically Leviticus, Exodus, Psalms and Ecclesiastes to find out. No matter what all this actually means in practice you have to pity the poor sod who having just bought the foreclosed house from the bank at a rock bottom price turns up all excited with his family only to find that there is someone else living there and who refuses to budge. And then to top it all he is the one who has to live like a bum in a camper van until such time the squatter is evicted. It's the American dream, you can't fault it.

☐ **Tick here when you have spotted the Savvy Squatter**

SYMPATHY RATING – 6
I have quite a lot of sympathy for the Savvy Squatter as when you put yourself in their shoes (metaphorically of course, as Lord knows what you might catch if you actually did so); you can see the logic of their actions. When faced with the stark choice of sleeping on the streets or using an empty home, what would you do? And if the banks can't be arsed to look after the houses which now belong to them, it's their problem and maybe that will teach them not to lend money to people who cannot or perhaps should not own a home in the first place.

RARITY – **3**

Unfortunately the 2001 census didn't include squatters so it is quite tricky to determine if the number of Savvy Squatters is growing, declining or staying much the same. All we know is that the number of empty homes is growing so whatever their number there will be plenty of houses to stay in.

WHAT ARE THEY DOING NOW?

Playing cat and mouse with the authorities and keeping one step ahead of the law as they break into their next property. And when it's time to move on, pooing on the carpet.

AVOIDANCE | REVENGE STRATEGIES

1. Although squatting is technically against the law, it is a shame that with so many properties lying empty that they can't be put to good use for the increasing number of homeless people that have nowhere else to go.

2. Set up an Estate Agency for Squatters. Advertise all the latest empty homes which could be accessed by the homeless on the internet (it's okay, they all have smart phones these days) and include a 'help and advice' section on how to break in, change the locks and deal with the police. As you will not be able to make any money from the squatters themselves, why not sell advertising to porn sites and make some money that way?

3. Establish an anti squatting vigilante service for the owners of empty properties. Charge £100 per property per month and to avoid unnecessary costs use cardboard cut-outs of Dobermans, riot police and famous film stars to deter would-be squatters. Consider offering a gardening service too so that they are ready for the upturn in the property market.

4. Air a new property programme called 'Squatter's Ladder' in which two teams of squatters have ten weeks to trade up from an empty one bedroomed maisonette to a deserted 15 bedroomed mansion. The winners will get to keep the mansion. The programme can be hosted by Colin and Justin to give it that camp edge.

5. If you really want to cash in, why not employ some bogus squatters to trash empty properties and then offer a refurbishment and repair service to the desperate banks. And if you are really smart, you should ensure all the squatters you employ are builders, carpenters, electricians and plumbers.

THE SAVVY SQUATTER:

☐ Can blame someone else for their predicament

☐ Only has them self to blame

☐ Deserves our sympathy and should be hugged

☐ Deserves our contempt and should be shot

The Secure Civil Servant

In the past, telling anyone that you worked for the government was tantamount to admitting you were a hobo. You see no one valued the civil servant as they were considered lazy good-for-nothing scroungers who really didn't want to get a proper job in the real world, either that or they were generally unemployable and only the government, as employer of the last resort, was willing to take them onto their books (sorry, our books). Tales of civil servants taking their sick leave as holiday entitlement; abusing the flexitime rules; soiling the toilets; and being perpetually on strike because they only wanted to work one day a week, are legend. On top of this was the litany of disasters which could only occur in the public sector; massive computer projects going completely wrong; bungled decisions and a focus on the pointless. Needless to say, this didn't do them any favours at all, especially when it came to attracting talent. The other thing of course is that most of them had such poor taste in clothing. Favouring tired-looking grey suits and brown shoes, most of them resembled peasants from the middle ages – well they were servants after all, so what should we expect? Being a civil servant was a career choice for many because it was safe, secure and didn't require much effort. And if you were incompetent enough you could eventually make it into the senior grades where you could do even more damage.

Over time and especially when the state became obsessed with political correctness and interfering with every aspect of our lives, (dictating to us about what we should eat, how we should drive and why it was important to be careful when crossing the road), the numbers of civil servants ballooned. And with this came a 'jobs bonanza'. Of course, as there were no real jobs to do, because that was what the private sector was there for, the civil servants in charge began to dream up pointless positions and job descriptions to fill the EU Work Directive's 35 hour week. Typical such 'non-jobs' included *Street Football Coordinator* (required to persuade feral youths on the local sink estate to kick the ball into the back of a net rather than through a pensioner's front window), *Community Space Challenger Coordinator* (needed to help single parents fit things into their cupboards which they were clearly challenged by), *Enviro-Crime Enforcement Officer* (getting people who let their dogs poo on the pavement to clear it up), *Befriending Coordinator* (to help the socially inept, privately educated and serial sociopaths make at least one friend that wasn't an animal), and *Mind and Nutrition Leader* (educating the masses on the important link between spirituality and eating and why red coloured food represents happiness and good karma). Each and every one of these jobs paid quite handsomely and didn't actually require the job holder to have any real skills or qualifications apart from being overly enthusiastic and cheerful.

As much as we can laugh at such stupid and pointless jobs, the last laugh is on us, the private sector employee who has become the new hobo. Today, being a civil servant is one of the best career choices you can make. You spot them still shopping at Marks and Spencer looking smug and confident and clutching the latest directive from central

office. Of course the other dead giveaway is their somewhat dishevelled look and poor dress sense – after all, you can take the civil servant out of the hobo, but you can never take the hobo out of the civil servant.

It should of course come as no surprise as to why so many people are currently scouring second-hand shops and jumble sales for grey suits and brown shoes and making a beeline for the nearest government building. The choice, they say is simple. If you want to get a half-decent job which requires you to work less than an Arts Student at a third-tier university, with guaranteed pay rises every year, even if you are crap at your job, (in fact if you are, you will more than likely get promoted), and with no danger of ever being made redundant, then it's the Civil Service for you. What's more, you get to enjoy the benefits of extra time off, which includes the Queen's Birthday, bonuses for *struggling* into work when it snows and not forgetting one of the few final salary pension schemes left in the whole world. And all of this comes at the taxpayer's expense, so no need to worry about shareholders, monthly sales targets, performance reviews or indeed anything remotely commercial. It's a no brainer. When the poor private sector employee is enduring pay freezes, pay cuts, reduced pension funding and the boot often with nothing more than a cardboard box as their severance package, the public servant can sit back in their dreary office feeling pretty damn good. For once playing it safe has paid off – they can still buy houses, still skip to work every day, take their sick leave as holiday and look forward a nice relaxing retirement secure in the knowledge that as long as everyone else is taxed to death, they can catch a few rays on a Spanish beach.

☐ **Tick here when you have spotted the Secure Civil Servant**

SYMPATHY RATING – **0**
The problem with the Secure Civil Servant is that no matter how hard they try to justify their existence and insist that they are doing a vitally important job, none of us believe them. It is difficult to sympathise with them when they claim their jobs are hard or that they are poorly paid. That might have worked 20 years ago, but not today when they are paid better than most private sector employees. Sure there might be one or two that do something useful, but this description tends to be restricted to nurses, doctors, surgeons, policemen, firemen and the like. The unfortunate thing of course is that for every useful public servant there are at least 100 who aren't.

RARITY – **7**
Something in the region of one in five people work in the public sector and in some places this is almost 100%. And as the recession grinds endlessly on, the number of people who can claim to be bona fide members of the Secure Civil Servant Club will undoubtedly grow. As for the private sector, most of them will be waiting for the axe to swing once more and figuring how best to spend their redundancy package – yes you've guessed it, down the charity shop.

WHAT ARE THEY DOING NOW?
Much the same as they always did, pretending to add some value to 'UK plc' as they shuffle a few papers around their desk and waste yet more billions on doing, well not much really.

AVOIDANCE | REVENGE STRATEGIES
1. Hang around strip joints and industrial estates as these are probably about the only two places left where you won't find a Secure Civil Servant these days.

2. Lecture them on the high levels of public waste and ask them to justify their existence, to you, the taxpayer *(aka their boss)*.

3. Establish an internet action group and start a protest with the slogan 'Public Sector Jobs for Private Sector Employees'.

4. Set up a government quango for generating non-jobs. Consider introducing such jobs as Bottom Inspector, Paint Peeling Community Champion and Compost Composition Consultant.

5. Run for Parliament, get elected and then introduce a new Bill which outsources all non-essential civil service jobs *(hmm, something like 90%)* to India; it will save a shed load of cash which you can then feed into tax cuts for all the hard pressed private sector workers *(those who still have jobs, that is)*.

THE SECURE CIVIL SERVANT:

☐ Can blame someone else for their predicament

☐ Only has them self to blame

☐ Deserves our sympathy and should be hugged

☐ Deserves our contempt and should be shot

The Self-help Sado

W hat is it about self-help that brings people back for more? Surely if all the books which crowd the bookshops were any good and the seminars at all effective, all you would need is one dose and you would be cured of whatever problem your might have and really become that new man or women you dreamt of being. It is obvious that something isn't working. Now it could be that the self-help books are a load of old cobblers and are merely selling snake oil to those too pathetic to pull themselves together. Or, maybe it's because the people that buy them have a plethora of problems that only the purchase of a whole library of titles could hope to cure. Or perhaps it's because the alternative is just too expense and too painful – all those therapy sessions, (the couch, the crying, the punching of pillows and all those goddamn tissues). Whatever the reason, some 693 million self-help books are sold every year and Americans, the most self-help obsessed nation on earth, spend in the region of $8 billion a year on self-help. Of course we all know that most self-help books and seminars are only designed to help you part with your hard earned cash. The true beneficiaries (and I don't count the reader in this) are the authors, publishers and bookshops who all make skip loads of cash in the process – who needs JK Rowling when you have self-help and a helpless audience, the perfect marriage if ever there was one.

The self-help industry has of course been fuelled by the obsession with status and wealth; and it caters for the lazy who hope that reading a book is somehow going to provide them with a shortcut to success. The subtext in all these books is that you may indeed be a lazy, good for nothing, workshy excuse for a human being, but you *deserve* to be rich, in the same way that the author of such tosh *deserves* to die. We all know that unless you happen to be wealthy, have very rich parents, are a pimp or perhaps well endowed you are going to have to work very hard to become relatively well off and even harder if you are going to be fabulously wealthy. Of course such self-help books are no use to anyone right now as the government is going to take any money you might make having read the book and applied all the valuable lessons. Still, you will be a better person inside.

Over the years self-help books have made more and more ridiculous promises both in their titles and their content. Most set out how you can become rich beyond your wildest dreams in 80 pages of bullet points, platitudes and obvious statements, such as 'Belieeeeeeeeve in yourself', 'write down a list of things you need to do today' and 'be nice to people; they will give you cash in return'. All very useful stuff I'm sure, but only if you happen to be a moron, but then it seems that there are a lot of morons around these days, especially if 693 million self-help books are sold every year. Then there are those which are set out like a child's story in which every day folk (or in one case, mice) find new found enthusiasm for work and wealth by talking to the happy-go-lucky chaps in a slaughterhouse mechanically recovering offal and other inedible parts of an animal's carcass. Others will tell the tale of a little boy called Gordon who wanted to be

an economic genius when he grew up and be loved by everyone in the whole world. It follows his life through boarding school where he was whipped to within an inch of his life and roasted on a spit on an open fire, his time at Oxford when he met his bosom bud Tony, a cheesy untrustworthy type, and finally to when he made it into power and was an economic genius, and everyone loved him. The books will provide you, the in need of self-help reader, the invaluable lessons which will make you love your work colleagues, become independently wealthy or indeed become a well-loved unelected Prime Minister.

The Self-help Sado is typically a weak-willed weakling without any backbone. Once they have read the latest self-help best seller, 'Pull your bloody socks up and make billions' they talk earnestly about the changes they are going to make in their lives. A few weeks later they are back in the same bookshop purchasing the latest clutch of crap looking for their next fix and latching onto this week's best seller 'Tighten up your belt and become an instant celebrity' in the belief that this is the one that will really change their life.

Of course, not to miss out in the newfound austerity associated with the recession and after recognising that all their crap books focused on making absolutely everyone in the world incredibly wealthy were no longer selling, our self-help friends are now making a packet by telling their readers how to survive the recession and how to still be rich by mugging the wealthy. People are flocking to seminars, online blogs and all manner of self-help websites which dish out a whole bunch of mindless advice that is nothing more than commonsense. Will they ever learn? I doubt it.

☐ **Tick here when you have spotted the Self-help Sado**

SYMPATHY RATING – **1**

It is impossible to have any sympathy for the Self-help Sado as they really ought to know better by now. If they are delusional enough to believe that reading a book is going to make them wealthy or watching some sharp-suited conman on stage for a few hours is really going to make a difference to the fact that they are an unemployed tap dancer without much prospect of finding work outside of the Panto season, then they deserve to be a failure. The simple answer is to save your money and spend it on something more useful, such as a razor blade, some tranquilisers, or a visa to leave the country along with everyone else.

RARITY – **6**

The recession is great for self-help because it is at times like this that people turn to anything to help them through the depression and pain that comes with economic Armageddon. Some turn to religion, and others to farm animals. But the majority turn to the latest self-help advice, including 'How to survive the 2007–3007 depression', by S. Hite PhD (and they always have a PhD ... probably in creative writing, but of course no one ever bothers to find out).

WHAT ARE THEY DOING NOW?
Still clutching at straws as they look for the next great wave of self-help literature because the last batch didn't quite do it for them. Bereft of any original thought and in need of a damn good slap, they wander endlessly through the bookshops of Britain in search of the self-help holy grail.

AVOIDANCE / REVENGE STRATEGIES
1. Steer clear of all self-help books as all they do is fuddle your brain, make you less self-reliant and create an addiction for yet more of them. If you really do need help, seek the advice of a trained professional, not someone who is good at hypnosis and party tricks.

2. Write a book entitled 'You can think yourself poor' in which you offer expert advice on how to fritter money away. Start by charging £75 a copy and consider putting an image of Gordon Brown on the front cover.

3. Hover around the self-help shelves of your local bookshop. When someone comes across to browse the many interesting titles, help yourself to their wallet.

4. Stage a massive self-help love-in event at a major location, such as Olympia. Call it something like 'Credit Crunch, my arse' and charge £209 per ticket. Make a massive entrance with lots of dry ice and fireworks and spend the next 32 hours talking a load of old cobblers, foaming at the mouth and mentioning as many famous people as you can. Make sure you record the event and sell the DVD (at a cool £345) to the idiots that attended, as well as those that didn't.

5. Start an online cosmic ordering service in which your Self-help Sados make their orders after paying you a reassuringly expensive fee. I suggest you use PayPal and make sure that you state categorically that all sales are final.

THE SELF-HELP SADO:

☐ Can blame someone else for their predicament

☐ Only has them self to blame

☐ Deserves our sympathy and should be hugged

☐ Deserves our contempt and should be shot

The Self-righteous Tightwad

During the Great Depression, things were pretty tough. Initiated by the precipitous drop in the stock market, the famous Wall Street Crash of 1929, the world-wide slump that followed led to deprivation beyond what any of us today could imagine; soup kitchens sprang up that had to cater for thousands, tented cities where those who had lost everything lived with their families, and millions of people eking out a living as best they could. And of course it led to the emergence of the National Socialist Party in Germany and ultimately World War II. So, all in all, the 1930s was a pretty bad decade to be alive.

According to some commentators, we are entering a new Depression which could be just as bad as the first one. Well, apart from the flat screen televisions, mobile phones, McDonald's restaurants, central heating, massive trillion Dollar bailouts, hot and cold running water and Madonna. It is time to start saving money and learning the lessons from the last Depression, such as:

- Making soup out of cockerel's feet which by all accounts was delicious and certainly more tasty than their testicles.

- Filling up a washtub full of rainwater and leaving it in the summer sun to warm up – a cheap alternative to taking an expensive bath or shower heated by electricity or gas.

- Talking long walks into the mountains to find the odd berry or two or if you are really lucky a bullfrog, or perhaps a squirrel – far more nutritious than a burger or a hotdog. Exercise too.

- Cutting up pictures from magazines and making papier-mâché frames to go round them as an alternative to spending millions of Dollars on an Old Master.

The people from the last Depression, well those that are still alive, are being tapped for their wealth of knowledge and expertise to help those who now need to cut back and learn to be far more careful with their money and resources. However, as much as some of us could no doubt benefit from the sage advice, there is one member of the community who could give them a run for their money, and that's the Self-righteous Tightwad who is coming into their own.

We all know of people who take pride on making a single teabag last 5000 years, or a pair of underpants last throughout adulthood, as well as those who refuse to buy you a pint of beer when you are down the pub on a Friday night. But the Self-righteous Tightwad takes money saving to a new plane now that the economy is going down the tubes; and they love it. Only they can have millions in the bank and still salvage bagel scraps left on their plates for pizza toppings, or cut shampoo bottles in half to get the last fluid ounce of liquid out of the container. Others pride themselves on replacing the already crazily cheap own brand fabric softener with vinegar (and you

thought they just worked in a fish and chip shop) or making their own detergent out of baking soda. One guy recently called into a radio show to inform the listeners how to cut back on electricity and water bills by stopping and starting their power shower in the morning. They would turn it on for no more than 30 seconds to get wet. Turn it off and soap them self down and then turn it back on again for another 30 seconds to wash all the soap off. And there's me spending 30 minutes in the shower – I clearly have a lot to learn. Others will wear their clothes until their arse is literally hanging out of their trousers and usually find themselves being marched to the local Primark or Wal-Mart to buy a new pair.

It seems that the Credit Crunch is bringing out the tightwad in us all. We now see investment bankers shopping at Wal-Mart (with some of them working there too – it must be the massive bonus that attracts them) and people making do with just two pairs of shoes instead of ten. Jumble sales are all the rage and the High Street is filling up with Pound stores and charity shops. What a welcome change from what we used to have – estate agents, building societies and banks.

☐ **Tick here when you have spotted the Self-righteous Tightwad**

SYMPATHY RATING – **3**
The Self-righteous Tightwad is harmless and is someone to be admired. If they really want to spend their lives cleaning their clothes with vinegar or using leftover bagels as pizza topping then good luck to them. The other good thing about them is that all the retailers out there and of course our politicians really, really hate the Self Righteous Tightwad; they would much rather we continue to spend our money unwisely in order to get the economy moving again. But the Tightwad is unrepentant – they revel in being tightwads and as far as they are concerned when it comes to the next Depression, it's a case of 'bring it on!'.

RARITY – **4**
Thankfully the Self Righteous Tightwad is quite rare, although we should expect their ranks to swell as purse strings get tighter. The majority keep themselves to themselves, hiding in discussed quarries and condemned housing. You will however see them by the sides of major roads and motorways where they wait eagerly for a passing lorry to kill the odd dog, cat, or rabbit and if they are very lucky, deer.

WHAT ARE THEY DOING NOW?
Fighting with hobos over the contents of dustbins in the side alleys of major conurbations. You will see hoards of them around the bins located outside fast food joints or those restaurants which are still in business. Nothing is sacred to them, and let's face it they could probably turn the half chewed food into a rather tasty three course meal for six.

AVOIDANCE | REVENGE STRATEGIES

1. It is very important to eke out as much as you can from the things you buy. Being thrifty should be a badge of honour that each and every one of us should wear in these difficult times.

2. Get a copy of 'The Ultimate Cheapskate's Roadmap to True Riches' – it is packed full of useful hints and tips on how to dress like a hobo and keep your purse firmly shut. If you don't like that, why not try that classic text 'Thrift' written by Samuel Smiles in 1879. In it he includes such gems as spend less than you earn; pay ready money, never run into debt and keep a regular account of all you earn'.

3. Scour magazines and websites for money-off coupons and use them to save you loads of money; see if you can live off less than £30 per week. And when you have finished, use the money you've saved to buy yourself a new Porsche.

4. Pose as a lottery agent and go round a Self-righteous Tightwad's house and inform them they have won ten million Pounds. Tell them that a condition of winning is for them to live the life of luxury and watch as they have a heart attack.

5. Write a road-kill cookbook in which you describe how nutritious meals can be made from a variety of dead animals and rodents you find squashed at the side of the road. If you are particularly ambitious why not open a road-kill supermarket?

THE SELF-RIGHTEOUS TIGHTWAD:

☐ Can blame someone else for their predicament

☐ Only has them self to blame

☐ Deserves our sympathy ad should be hugged

☐ Deserves our contempt and should be shot

The Taxed to Death

During the 1970s, the country was run by a bunch of fatheaded incompetent leftist fools hell-bent on destroying the country by imposing death defying tax rates and spending recklessly on the public sector. They almost succeeded and it was only due to the kind heartedness of the International Monetary Fund (IMF) that they didn't. Of course, being bailed out by the IMF was pretty much admitting that they had cocked up royally and were no better at running the country than a despotic failed state run by a lunatic more interested in lining their own pockets than running an efficient market driven economy. Today the country is run by a bunch of fatheaded incompetent leftist fools hell-bent on destroying the nation by imposing death defying tax rates and recklessly spending on the public sector. This time however, the IMF is so busy bailing out the rest of the world that they may actually succeed.

Although Benjamin Franklin may have said in a letter to Jean-Baptiste Leroy in 1789, 'in this world nothing can be said to be certain, except death and taxes' he actually got it wrong, as these days it seems that we can delay death far more effectively than in the past. The same, of course, cannot be said of taxes. Whilst non-stop bailouts abound, debt is spiralling out of control and will be reaching unsustainable levels within the next five minutes. The largesse of government knows no bounds and no matter where you are in the world, they are printing money, nationalising banks and paying the bonuses and pensions of corrupt CEOs like it is going out of fashion. Of course we know that all this will need to be paid back once the recession, depression or whatever it turns out to be is over and you've guessed it, it's going to be you and I that pay – and oh boy, are we going to pay. Unless you happen to be a friend of a high ranking politician or a tax evader (although this is getting less popular these days as tax authorities finally realise that too many exceptionally rich individuals are paying less tax than someone on benefits), then you know that you are going to spend the rest of your life paying for the government's almighty screw-up.

Naturally, the tax raising ability of the government is well known; they are masters of the art of raising tax whilst publicly claiming that they aren't. Indeed governments have even been elected because they stated they would never, ever, ever raise taxes. Of course we all know this is a lie (after all that's a politician's core competency) and they kept their fingers crossed when they said it, so technically it didn't count. In all there have been 157 'non-tax rises' (euphemistically termed 'stealth taxes' because we are apparently so utterly stupid that we won't realise) including the raid on pensions (not a tax rise), the increases in National Insurance (not a tax rise), the cap on tax free allowances (not a tax rise) and so on. We can be sure that these will be joined by many more as the government runs out of options to address the fiscal cock-up, including at last some genuine tax rises. Of course, as taxes continue to increase, people, and especially the middle classes, are going to get increasingly angry and vociferous. Some will take to the streets; others will try dirty protests in their local branch of Her Majesty's Revenue & Customs and a few will sew their mouths up with fishing tackle.

The Taxed to Death is typically red faced, very angry and on the brink of a seizure. They spit nails when anyone mentions tax, the recession or the government and go off on a 30 minute tirade, marching up and down, spewing profanities as they go. Faced with years of penury, they have to decide whether to leave the country or just stand by and watch as the tax they pay is just pissed away. They are not alone, as people are already stirring in our former colony, the United States, where disgruntled taxpayers have been holding the latter day equivalent of the Boston Tea Party. Of course, unlike the real event which involved incredible levels of bloodshed, the wrath of King George III, and the military discipline of the Red Coats, this one is tame by comparison and will have absolutely no impact at all. Plus, of course, no tea is involved. I suppose we have to give them points for trying. At least in the UK we know how to have a damn good riot.

☐ **Tick here when you have spotted the Taxed to Death (I suggest you look in the mirror)**

SYMPATHY RATING – **9**
Let's face it none of us want to pay tax, but we recognise that some taxation is inevitable if we are going to maintain a stable society. However, when our tax is being wasted on harebrained government projects which stand no chance of ever being successful, funding the greed of money grabbing politicians who feel that their criminal application of lax expense policies is somehow justifiable, or paying for the non-jobs of civil servants, then things are clearly getting out of hand. Knowing that taxes will rise and rise and rise for the next few thousand years is not only depressing but will ultimately result in those with any sense leaving the country. So in terms of sympathy, then it has to be high. Mind you, all those greedy bastards out there such as bankers, CEOs and milkmen, well they can pay up and deserve no sympathy whatsoever.

RARITY – **10**
Given that public-sector debt is so out of control and will soon be above 100% of GDP, the number people who could be considered to be a bonafide member of the Taxed to Death Club will increase exponentially. And it won't be long before we are seeing near 100% tax rates on any earnings over £30 – it's the only way that we will be able to get through this mess. Naturally, it might be best if we all became state employees, as at least then you will be safe in the knowledge that all the taxes are being spent on you.

WHAT ARE THEY DOING NOW?
Collecting images of politicians and their local tax officials and taping them to dart boards. In addition to venting their spleen in non-violent ways, they spend hours and hours moaning and griping about how much tax they pay and how much better off we would be if we lived under Edward IV who didn't raise taxes at all

(well only after he had won the Battle of Tewkesbury in 1471 and realised that he had better keep his nose clean if he was going to survive).

 AVOIDANCE | REVENGE STRATEGIES
1. Accept that no matter who's in power you are going to pay a shed load more tax – better get used to living like a peasant and eating turnips then and wearing lots of woolly jumpers in the winter.

2. Emigrate to a low tax country such as the British Virgin Islands where you will pay no tax at all.

3. Find yourself a very good accountant who will proffer you some very sound (and no doubt illegal) advice which will allow you to avoid paying excessive amounts of tax.

4. Get a copy of Yaz and the Plastic Population's 1988 smash hit 'The Only Way is Up' and play it loudly near any politician or tax official.

5. Write to the Chancellor and recommend that he starts to tax poo. It would be simple to administer (through a simple weights and measures device inserted in the U-bend) and given that everyone has to take a dump every now and then this would be an easy way to pay off the outstanding government debt. What's more there could be some interesting new jobs emerging from the newly-formed 'Brown Economy', including poo analyser, poo-measurement device installation engineer and scatological consultant. This will also give a whole new meaning to the notion of having a shit job.

THE TAXED TO DEATH:

☐ Can blame someone else for their predicament

☐ Only has them self to blame

☐ Deserves our sympathy

☐ Deserves our contempt

The Unabashed Bankrupt

The Italians have given us much to be grateful for: the Renaissance, the Sistine Chapel, the Roman Occupation, the Mafia and of course the Catholic Church. But their most significant gift to the world has been the banking system. Even though I doubt that many people will feel grateful right now, there is one aspect to it about which I am sure the many thousands of people whose finances are completely blown will be delighted. You see, the Italians invented the term bankrupt, although to be fair they did this when they used to be both economically and geopolitically important; had they done it today no one would have taken any notice. The term comes from the Italian word meaning broken bench. Apparently an ancient custom called for the breaking of benches or tables of bankers and money lenders whose businesses had failed. I do wonder if the tables were broken on the heads or perhaps the backs of the failed businessmen, but since there are no records we can only speculate.

Since introducing the term a few hundred years ago, it has been embraced with real vigour although in the UK we view bankrupts as pariahs, the US treats them like returning war heroes. In fact, if you haven't been made bankrupt at least once then you just aren't American. Irrespective of how you might be treated, it is important to understand that there is always the risk of going bust when embarking on any business venture, so it is necessary to give people a second chance. Which is why the law does not kill those who have been made bankrupt, even though their creditors would love to.

There are plenty of people who are now going down the tubes purely and simply because they can no longer maintain their 24 x 7 spending binge. Such people, the Unabashed Bankrupt as they are known in government circles, have not managed their finances at all well and have spent well beyond what little means they had. Over the last decade the number of people going bankrupt has steadily increased and since it became both fashionable and easy to run up a huge mountain of debt and then just walk away from it, the numbers have ballooned. And now that we are in full recessionary flight we are seeing unprecedented numbers of people going bankrupt – something in the region of 5000 a day are expected to go to the wall between now and the end of next week.

The Unabashed Bankrupt is clearly someone who was incapable of living within a budget, trading within their means or able to tot up their spending correctly so at least they could see the mess they were getting themselves into. Instead, they carried on spending oblivious to the consequences and ignoring all the calls from the credit card and loan companies by either pretending to be Chinese or a retard. Somehow it didn't matter as there was always another card or loan company who was more than happy to pick up the slack and they knew in the back of their mind that when it all got too much, they declare bankruptcy. Of course being clever they would wait until the amount of debt they had was greater than their lifetime earnings (including pay rises, bonuses, job moves and promotions) before they threw in the towel. Helped along by one of the

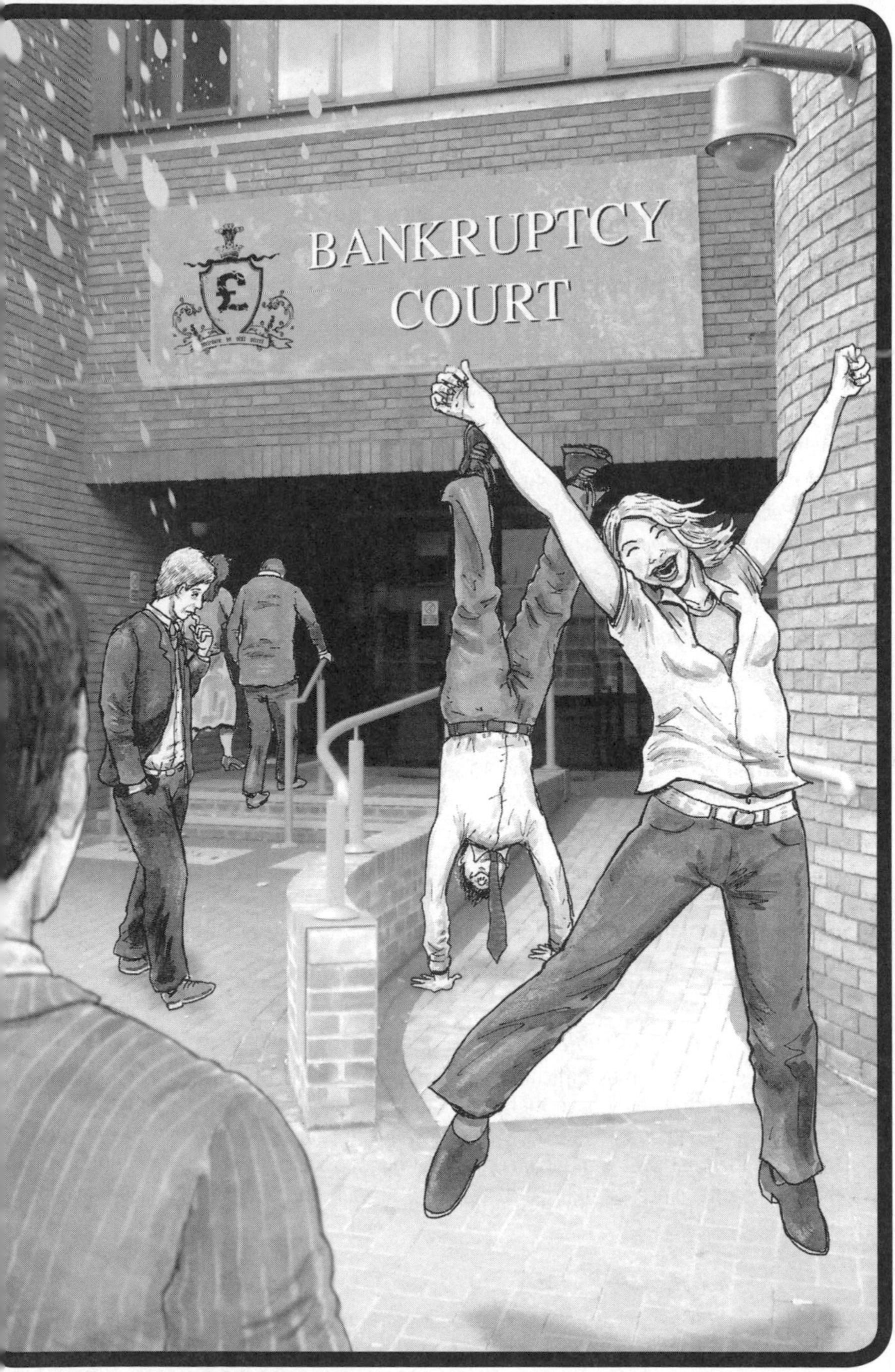
BANKRUPTCY
COURT

many debt counselling adverts, they would be persuaded that bankruptcy was for them. So off they went and sought professional help from one of the many ambulance chasing companies which specialise in helping the overspent go bankrupt. Offering you a simple one stop shop to kick all your debts into touch and walk away, they make it look so simple; on line forms, a brief court appearance, no more debt and you can finally get some sleep again. All for a flat rate fee of £87.

Apparently the bankruptcy law splits the Unabashed Bankrupt into one of three categories:

- *The Savvy Student* who having completed their degree feels that they shouldn't have to pay for their education (after all that's what toffs do, not the working class) and considers it unfair that they don't have much to show for it all apart from a certificate which doesn't even have their name spelt correctly. It wouldn't be so bad if they had a car, television, fancy stereo and other stuff, but unfortunately they don't.

- *The Bankrupt Beauty* who unable to control her insatiable urge to buy overpriced clothes, jewellery, shoes, toiletries, handbags, watches, and celebrity magazines has found that she has no money left and has decided that going on the game won't make much difference to her financial situation.

- *The Consumed Consumer* who has exhausted every single credit line available to them and has given up playing credit card roulette with the 124 cards they own.

It is interesting to watch people snake in and bound out of the bankruptcy court. On the way in, they resemble Atlas with the world's debt on their shoulders – sad, crumpled and worried to death; then after the 30 second court hearing they come out, punch the air and do the occasional handstand, delighted that they are free at last.

Although we may all dismiss the reckless behaviour of the Unabashed Bankrupt, be appalled at their crass behaviour at just walking away from their debt and boast that we would never fall into the same trap, we should remember that we are living in a bankrupt nation and are all therefore technically up to our eyeballs in debt.

☐ **Tick here when you have spotted the Unabashed Bankrupt**

SYMPATHY RATING – **3**

It is generally difficult to feel sympathy for the Unabashed Bankrupt, after all they only have themselves to blame. If only they had spent some time watching back-to-back episodes of 'Life Laundry' they might have realised that their spending was somehow compensating for a deficiency in their childhood that they had long since buried, and as a result perhaps they might have avoided bankruptcy.

RARITY – **7**

With record numbers of people going bankrupt it is highly likely that you will know someone who has and it might even be you. Unfortunately they can be difficult to spot because as yet the bill that will force bankrupts to wear a blond afro wig and square badge with a broken pound sign on it has yet to pass through the House of Lords, although it is imminent.

WHAT ARE THEY DOING NOW?

Realising that going bankrupt wasn't such a breeze after all. Despite all the helpful advice from the company that assisted them, have found out that amongst a long list of things they lose control of their assets; they cannot obtain credit for over £250 without the permission of the lender; they cannot act as a company director; they may not become a member of Parliament and they may be publicly examined in court which sounds very painful. Still, once they have been discharged they could give it another go.

AVOIDANCE | REVENGE STRATEGIES

1. Avoid all the traps of becoming a bankrupt – spending money you haven't got, being a student, being a woman, being a man, losing your job, running a business, buying a car, buying a house, getting married, getting divorced, having children, adopting children and watching test cricket.

2. If you are thinking about going bankrupt, why not try an Individual Voluntary Agreement instead. It is less draconian than bankruptcy – you still get to write off most of your debts and you can keep you home too.

3. Have some t-shirts printed with the caption 'I visited the Bankruptcy Court and all I got was this lousy T-shirt' and hang around county courts ready to sell them to the newly bankrupt (cash only of course). Priced carefully, you will probably do well and the bankrupts will have something to remember the hearing by.

4. Set-up a social networking site called Bankrupts Reunited which brings everyone who has ever been bankrupted together and allows them to exchange stories and perhaps if they are very lucky, more than that.

5. Create a new advert for people thinking about going bankrupt with the slogan 'Racked up way too much debt? Happy to be considered a pariah? Then call Dig-Yourself-Out-of-Debt-Now where one of our friendly UK-based call centre staff will help you stick two fingers up at your creditors. It's fast; it's cheap and it's chic. Call today!'.

THE UNABASHED BANKRUPT:

☐ Can blame someone else for their predicament

☐ Only has them self to blame

☐ Deserves our sympathy and should be hugged

☐ Deserves our contempt and should be shot

The Worthless Degree Holder

Education, Education, Education, you just can't fault it. It makes perfect sense that everyone should have a reading age of more than a seven year old and be able to write their name in joined up writing. Moreover, without a good, solid and ideally free education (only the inbred, social climbing middle classes and idiots tend to pay for it), how on earth do you think the next generation will get on in the modern workplace with all that technology? How can we expect them to remain employed so that they can pay the huge amounts of taxes that are coming their way, and most critically be able to read something more demanding than 'The Sun' every morning unless they are educated?

During the last real recession in the early 1980s when there were riots in the streets and millions were left unemployed (hmm, sounds quite like today), the manufacturing heart of the country was ripped clean out by Messer's Thatcher and Tebbit. As the years went by and as the economy recovered, fewer and fewer things had the 'Made in Britain' logo on it, which was probably just as well given most of it was crap and fell apart anyway. This left everyone rushing headlong into the brave new world of the 'Service Economy'. Everyone was getting the message; no one wanted to get their hands dirty anymore (well apart from the millions of immigrants who were more than happy to push their arm around the U-bend) and everyone wanted jobs with important titles, like *window-cleaning consultant*, or *hairstyle engineer*. It was believed that only those who possessed a good education, and ideally a clutch of degrees would succeed. So the idea was to ditch the old University and Polytechnic system and make everything beyond a playschool a university. And it wasn't long before public toilets and schools for the mentally challenged became universities along with the old polytechnics, zoos, churches, and kebab vans, in fact anything that could be loosely classed as an educational establishment. As these dog-shit universities, as they are colloquially known, spewed forth their newly minted graduates there was just one snag. Each and every one of them was holding a piece of paper that told the world they had a worthless degree. What the government (who remain obsessed with everyone getting a degree, no matter how utterly useless it is) failed to tell the poor sods is that having a degree in tap dancing, media studies, the history of art, politics, ancient Babylonian legal texts for the hard of hearing, or films in which John Wayne shot people with his non-writing hand is completely pointless and of no practical use to anyone. Now that you can get degrees in burger flipping from fast food joints, or shelf-stacking from supermarkets, it is clear anyone can get a degree and most are not worth the paper they are written on.

As they throw their mortarboards high into the summer sky after three long, hard years of study (well, OK, spending most of their time in the Union Bar getting wrecked on Pernod because they only have one or two hours of lectures a week) they all talk excitedly about how they are going to land a top job and change the world. They've joined

the elite ranks of the graduate community and believe they have finally made it. It doesn't take long for reality to set in and the realisation that their fantastically cutting edge degree is as much use as a crap flavoured lollipop. Finding that they are under qualified for any job that actually requires useful skills, they end up as an Estate Agent or working on a sub-assembly production line fixing plastic turds to baseball caps for the export market.

In these politically correct times where everyone needs to be included and the taking part is more important than winning, and in which everyone is 'special' (well, special needs anyway), our Worthless Degree Holders all seem to have first class honours. The reason why is patently obvious to anyone with more than a peanut inside their skull. Most degrees are the equivalent of a watered down CSE in woodwork where the examiners award maximum marks for any substandard rubbish because the candidate attempted at least some of the questions and used a nice coloured pen to write their answers. It would surprise no one to hear that the millions of immigrants working in this country are better qualified than our media-hungry, iPod wearing, semi-literate graduates. It's no wonder most of them are going back home. And now that the recession is in full swing it seems everyone wants to go to university to avoid the dole queue. Just a couple of snags with this plan though. First, there aren't enough places to go round (because the government got their calculations wrong … again); second, the amount of money you will need to get through the course is going to be substantial. Finally, there is no guarantee that you will get a job at the end of it. Choose wisely now, won't you.

☐ **Tick here when you have spotted the Worthless Degree Holder,**

SYMPATHY RATING – 4
It's difficult to feel sympathetic about the poor Worthless Degree Holder; I think pity might be a better emotion. It's sad that they bought into the whole university thing and then decided to choose to pursue a degree in such pointless subjects. I guess the majority of them really believed the politicians when they told them it would make a difference to their career. It did, of course; it placed them firmly on top of the scrap heap. They would have been better off going to work and buying a £6.99 book on their chosen subject (they would have learned a lot more in the process no doubt). I guess the only thing that is annoying is the way they insist on putting BSc (Hons) after their name, like it actually means something when they are trying to sell you a three-bed semi in Skipton.

RARITY – 9
The Worthless Degree Holder is especially common right now as all the employers who would have embraced anyone with a pulse have either gone bust or contracted to the point where they only need good people and those who don't have an overinflated view of what they are worth. And as the recession drags on

they will soon be joined by another clutch of fresh faced, näive graduates all expecting to land plum (or is it bum) jobs. Still, there is one area of the employment market that still appreciates the varied skills which they have, and that's government.

WHAT ARE THEY DOING NOW?
Desperate to show the world that they have some useful skills and that they are as clever as their sad pushy parents led them to believe, they are busy appearing on any talent show that will take them, such as 'The Apprentice'. Of course, as we all know, it just makes them look even more incompetent and you can guarantee that they will never be employed again.

AVOIDANCE | REVENGE STRATEGIES
1. Never discuss qualifications with anyone. It's like religion, sex, politics and housing – taboo subjects which only end up with someone getting glassed.

2. Start a campaign to raise the standards of tertiary education and start by demanding that only proper degrees are awarded.

3. Play them the Jam song 'When You're Young' making sure you turn up the volume when it gets to 'the world is your oyster, but your future's a clam'.

4. Set up your own university, offering a range of interesting degree subjects, such as worm casts of the Middle East and the expenses policies of New Labour.

5. Invite them into your well-appointed office or library with your certificates from Oxford University, The London School of Economics and MIT Sloan hanging on the wall and ask them where they studied and what degree they've got. When they answer look at them with a mix of compassion and disdain.

THE WORTHLESS DEGREE HOLDER:

☐ Can blame someone else for their predicament

☐ Only has them self to blame

☐ Deserves our sympathy and should be hugged

☐ Deserves our contempt and should be shot

Afterword - The Blame Game

A popular game in the early part of the Great War was 'The Blame Game' in which troops on the frontline would while away the hours before the next big push trying to figure out who had got them into the stupid war in the first place. Because board games were banned from the frontline, the soldiers had to make do with pencil and paper, and the occasional white flag came in handy every now and then. It was a very simple game.

Two columns were drawn up on either side of the page and a list of who could be blamed was added to each side. The soldiers would then determine who could blame who. For example, Kaiser Wilhelm could blame Gavrilo Princip (the guy who shot Archduke Ferdinand which started the chain reaction that led to mobilisation and war), whilst Gavrilo Princip could blame Franz Ferdinand (who wasn't listening to the demands from the Black Hand Gang and had to be taken out in order to make a statement about Serbian Independence) and so on. Apparently it kept them happy for hours and took their mind off the snipers, the weather, the poor sanitation and the incompetence of the generals who were regularly sending them off to their deaths.

To help illustrate how the game worked, I have included an example that was dug up around the Somme in 1921.

Kaiser Wilhelm	Kaiser Wilhelm
Archduke Franz Ferdinand	Archduke Franz Ferdinand
The Pope	The Pope
King George	King George
The Black Hand Gang	The Black Hand Gang
Gavrilo Princip	Gavrilo Princip
The Entente Cordiale	The Entente Cordiale
The Germans	The Germans
The Russians	The Russians
The Railway System	The Railway System

Now you have got the hang of it, you can do the same for the recession. Armed with the 50 frightful people contained within this book you will be able to spend hours with your friends and family playing the 'Blame Game' as your ancestors did all those years ago. You may want to recreate the list on a flipchart and use it at parties, barn dances and during political campaigns. And to help you along the way, I have included a page already for you to start playing.

And finally please remember the Five Golden Rules for Pain Spotting; they will help you live a fulfilled, happy and enriched life.

1. *NEVER JUDGE A BOOK BY ITS COVER*
You mustn't be fooled by initial appearances. What at first glance may seem like a Dubai Deserter may in fact turn out to be a Savvy Squatter who hasn't bothered to wash for a while. Likewise, a straightforward Cohabiting Divorcee may in fact be an Extended (to breaking point) Family member. First impressions count, sure, but exchanging views with a Buy-to-Let Loser might be somewhat damaging to your financial health.

2. *DON'T PIGEONHOLE*
Pains, like all other species on the planet and according to Darwin, are able to adapt, evolve, mutate and cross-fertilise, occasionally leaving you with a slippery, chameleon-like being to contend with. In this way, an Out of Touch Politician may also be a Gravy Train Politician (in fact it is highly likely that they will), a Financial Oracle a part-time Ponzi Schemer, and so on. There's nothing to stop you ticking off more than one 'Pain' per observation. So do your analysis, and be sure you have got all the qualities of every Pain straight before committing yourself.

3. *DON'T BE TOO JUDGMENTAL*
The reasons for this are two-fold. First off, this book is about providing an amusing diversion during the multi-year recession. Second, we are all Pains of one form or another, and as the saying goes, 'People in glasshouses shouldn't evade their taxes'.

4. *DON'T GET INTO ANY FIST-FIGHTS*
Any suggestions that 'the book told me to do it' are like a tower of jelly – they won't stand up in a court of law. It might work for politicians, but everyone hates them, so it doesn't count.

5. *LEARN TO LOVE YOUR PAIN*
This is the trickiest and most testing of all the Golden Rules. But you should learn to love the Pain. For he is your brother. Or your Bailout Beggar. The Bible tells us to love thy neighbour. And that means 'unconditionally'. Even when you want to beat the living daylights out of them. Besides, if you don't learn to love them, you might just go mad.

The Blame Game

The Bailout Beggar	The Bailout Beggar
The Buy-to-Let Basket Case	The Buy-to-Let Basket Case
The Cash Finder	The Cash Finder
The Celebrity Money Saver	The Celebrity Money Saver
The Cohabiting Divorcee	The Cohabiting Divorcee
The Conspicuous Consumer	The Conspicuous Consumer
The Credit Crunch Crook	The Credit Crunch Crook
The Credit Crunch Scrounger	The Credit Crunch Scrounger
The Deadbeat Debtor	The Deadbeat Debtor
The Desperate Estate Agent	The Desperate Estate Agent
The Disposed of Worker	The Disposed of Worker
The Downwardly Mobile	The Downwardly Mobile
The Dubai Deserter	The Dubai Deserter
The Economic Rioter	The Economic Rioter
The Economically Stressed	The Economically Stressed
The Elusive Tax Evader	The Elusive Tax Evader
The Escaping Entrepreneur	The Escaping Entrepreneur
The Ex, Expat	The Ex, Expat
The Extended (to breaking point) Family	The Extended (to breaking point) Family
The Financial Oracle	The Financial Oracle
The Frightened Fat Cat	The Frightened Fat Cat
The Good Lifer	The Good Lifer
The Gravy Train Politician	The Gravy Train Politician
The Grumpy Undergraduate	The Grumpy Undergraduate
The Humbled (but still incredibly wealthy) Bank Boss	The Humbled (but still incredibly wealthy) Bank Boss
The I'm About to Retire (but no longer can) Retiree	The I'm About to Retire (but no longer can) Retiree
The Irate Investor	The Irate Investor
The Living Big Loser	The Living Big Loser
The Low Bonus Banker	The Low Bonus Banker
The Miserable Middleclass	The Miserable Middleclass
The Newly Liberated	The Newly Liberated
The No Responsibility Regulator	The No Responsibility Regulator
The Not so Quite Master of the Universe	The Not so Quite Master of the Universe
The Nuevo Altruist	The Nuevo Altruist
The Organic Food Fly-by-night	The Organic Food Fly-by-night
The Out of Touch Politician	The Out of Touch Politician
The Outbound Immigrant	The Outbound Immigrant

The Petty Thief	The Petty Thief
The Pissed-off State Pensioner	The Pissed-off State Pensioner
The Ponzi Schemer	The Ponzi Schemer
The Pseudo Rich	The Pseudo Rich
The Relegated Rich	The Relegated Rich
The Repossessed	The Repossessed
The Savvy Squatter	The Savvy Squatter
The Secure Civil Servant	The Secure Civil Servant
The Self-help Sado	The Self-help Sado
The Self Righteous Tightwad	The Self Righteous Tightwad
The Taxed to Death	The Taxed to Death
The Unabashed Bankrupt	The Unabashed Bankrupt
The Worthless Degree Holder	The Worthless Degree Holder